THE MESSAGE, THE SPEAKER, THE AUDIENCE

McGRAW-HILL SERIES IN SPEECH

John J. O'Neill, Consulting Editor in Speech Pathology

THE MESSAGE, THE SPEAKER, THE AUDIENCE

Third Edition

John Hasling
Foothill College

McGraw-Hill Book Company
New York   St. Louis   San Francisco
Auckland   Bogotá   Hamburg   Johannesburg
London   Madrid   Mexico   Montreal
New Delhi   Panama   Paris   São Paulo
Singapore   Sydney   Tokyo   Toronto

THE MESSAGE, THE SPEAKER, THE AUDIENCE

6 7 8 9 0 DODO 8 9 8 7 6

ISBN 0-07-026995-5

This book was set in Optima by
World Composition Services, Inc.
The editors were Marian D. Provenzano,
Scott Amerman, and Barry Benjamin;
the designer was Robin Hessel;
the production supervisor was Rosann E. Raspini.
R. R. Donnelley & Sons Company was printer and
binder.

Library of Congress Cataloging in Publication Data

Hasling, John.
    The message, the speaker, the audience.

    (McGraw-Hill series in speech)
    Second ed. published in 1976 as: The audience,
the message, the speaker.
    Includes index.
    1. Public speaking. I. Title. II. Series.
PN4121.H267   1982   808.5'1   81-13693
ISBN 0-07-026995-5   AACR2
ISBN 0-07-026996-3 (instructors manual)

CONTENTS

PREFACE

Those who have used this text in its first edition are aware that I have returned to the original organizational pattern, starting with the message rather than the audience. I have done so because I believe that while audience analysis is an important consideration, the preparation of the message is fundamental and affords the most logical starting point for the beginning course in public speaking. Before students can think about either delivery or audience reception, they need to have in mind an idea of the message they want to send. Most students find that construction of the speech is the challenging part of the course and the sooner they get started on that aspect of the subject, the more sense they are able to make out of the rest of it.

The basic philosophy of the book remains the same. I want students to learn to communicate as much as they can in the least amount of time. Accomplishing this does not mean taking shortcuts in development, but structuring the speech so that it is understandable to the audience and fulfills the purpose that the speaker intended. The chapter on organization is still the focal point of the text because over the years my observation has been that students who speak best are those who have learned to arrange their ideas in a coherent outline.

This revision contains some new material as well as reorganization of the old. I have changed many of the examples and replaced them with others that are more current. I have updated the references and modified some of the language and terminology. In addition, there are several new concepts. One is *cognitive restructuring*—a methodology designed to help students deal with the problem of speech anxiety.

In all three editions emphasis has been placed on the assertion that the *message is the message received*. In other words, the way the listener perceives the message is the way it is, regardless of what the sender intended. The first two editions dealt exclusively with communication from the point of view of the speaker; the third edition includes the perspective of the listener. I have taken a cue from people in business corporations who have begun to realize the importance of this aspect of communication. Somehow we had come to believe that if one used good delivery techniques, was well organized, and had pertinent information, the message would be received accurately—and if it were not, the speaker had done something wrong. We know now that if misunderstandings are to be avoided, listeners must implement their own skills and take their share of the responsibility. We know too that we can identify the skills of listening and teach them just as we can teach the skills of speaking well. The important observation here is that the framework for listening well is the *mirror image* of that for effective speaking. When students become aware of their own weaknesses in listening, they can conclude that others may experience similar characteristics. And with this understanding they are better able to send messages in a way that overcomes those gaps in perception that are common to almost everyone.

The third edition stresses the obvious truth that communication does not take place at all unless someone is listening, and the speaker's job is to facilitate that process.

John Hasling

© 1980 United Feature Syndicate, Inc.

THE MESSAGE,
THE SPEAKER,
THE AUDIENCE

1

INTRODUCTION TO SPEECH COMMUNICATION

Today may be a day when you are going to stand up and speak to a group of people. The chances are that the decision to do so did not come upon you suddenly. More likely it was some time ago when you agreed to make the presentation and you have therefore had an opportunity to plan and prepare. It is probably also true that you were not motivated by a burning desire to give a speech, but rather that you had something that you wanted to communicate to other people. From this observation we can conclude that public speaking is not an end in itself but a *means* to an end. It is a vehicle we use when there is a lot of information we wish to convey in a short period of time to a small or large group of people. You may not perceive yourself as a speaker, but an occasion may arise when you feel you have something important to say—to give directions, to advocate a cause, to share an experience. Under these circumstances the most expedient style of communication is public speaking.

For a great many people giving a speech is a fearful experience, and some choose not to do it at all. Unfortunately often those who decline to speak are the ones who have the most valuable information. Consequently important and meaningful ideas are left unsaid.

The people who do choose to speak are not necessarily the ones with superior knowledge and information, but those who are willing to express what they think. Facility of oral expression is not dependent upon the value of thoughts or the significance of ideas. Communication is a variable of its own and needs to be studied independently of other disciplines. The art of verbal expression is sometimes called *rhetoric* and was first eloquently addressed by Aristotle.

> *Rhetoric may be defined as the faculty of observing in any given case the available means of persuasion. This is not a function of any other art. Every other art can instruct or persuade about its own particular subject-matter. But rhetoric we look upon as the power of observing the means of persuasion on almost any subject presented to us; and that is why we say that, in its technical character, it is not concerned with any special or definite class of subjects.*[1]

THE HISTORY OF RHETORIC

As soon as human beings became aware of the fact that their communication was unique among those of all the animals, there was a constant effort to examine it, analyze it, and improve upon it. "The ancient world knew well the overwhelming power of

[1] *The Rhetoric and Poetics of Aristotle,* trans. W. Rhys Roberts, Modern Library, New York, 1954, p. 24.

the word. Along about 2080 B.C. an aging pharaoh gave some advice to the son, Merykare, who would succeed him: 'Be a craftsman in speech, (so that) you mayest be strong.... the tongue is a sword ... and speech is more valorous than any fighting.' "[2]

These words had little practical application at the time, however, since Pharaoh was not a man to permit members of the general population to make speeches in the public square. It was, in fact, another 2000 years before there appeared the social forms conducive to the study of rhetoric. The first noteworthy text on public speaking was written by the Greek scholar Corax around 460 B.C. At this time the Greek city-states were experimenting with a democratic form of government, and a court system was established which allowed accused persons to plead their cases before an assembly. However, they were not permitted to have anyone else speak for them; they had to address the assembly themselves. Those who were not skilled in public speaking would go to teachers such as Corax for help in preparing their speeches. For the benefit of his students Corax worked out a system of organizing the speech and a method of argumentation. He was the first to postulate the three basic divisions we now call the *introduction,* the *body,* and the *conclusion.*

Corax and those who followed him were known as *sophists.* Some were highly principled and skilled. Others, such as Gorgias, were more concerned with an eloquent style of delivery than with the truth of their arguments. They taught that the art of persuasion lay in the way people spoke rather than in what they said. As more and more speakers began to employ grandiloquent oratory as a substitute for truth and knowledge, the sophists fell into poor repute. In fact the present meaning of the word "sophistry" is "plausible but faulty reasoning." It is interesting to note that two other words from that same root are "sophisticated" and "sophomore."

This period of history, known as the Age of Pericles, saw many contributions to the art of rhetoric. Much of the philosophy articulated at that time formed the foundation of our present theories. One of the most influential scholars of this period was Isocrates, who maintained that truth was paramount in any

---

[2] "Ebla, Splendor of an Unknown Empire," *National Geographic,* December 1978, p. 750.

oration, but that style was a legitimate means of persuading the listener to recognize the truth. Like Gorgias, he taught that a speech should be as well-styled as the speaker could make it. However, he cautioned his students to employ only those proofs that they honestly believed:

> *The same arguments we use in public we employ when*
> *we deliberate our own thoughts.*

Oratory was classified at this time as *forensic,* or argumentative; *deliberative,* or policy making; and *epideictic,* or eulogistic. The father of forensics was Protagoras, who insisted that his students be able to argue both sides of any issue. This is still a basic principle of debate. In most debate courses students are required to take first the affirmative and then the negative side of the proposition. The theory is that unless one is familiar with the arguments on both sides, one has no right to hold an opinion.

The most significant contribution to the art of rhetoric was made by Aristotle. The principles he outlined in 336 B.C. underlie everything that has been written since on the subject of public speaking, and his treatise *The Rhetoric* is still used as a text in colleges all over the world. Aristotle provided us with the first model of the three basic components of communication—the *speaker,* the *message,* and the *audience.* His thesis was that all three of these components must be present for any communication to take place. This may seem an elementary observation, but as we shall see, it is actually quite complex.

THE COMPONENTS OF COMMUNICATION

Aristotle's basic model of communication has since been expanded by the contributions of other great and learned men. Sigmund Freud's theories of personality gave insight into the way people react; John Dewey provided structure to the message with his model for reflective thinking; Marshall McLuhan hypothesized that the "medium is the message." These ideas and many others are incorporated into the modern theories of communication. Whereas Aristotle viewed rhetoric as an *art,* we tend to see it now more as an *experience.* The three basic components are not separate and distinct entities. Rather they are inextricably interwoven; communication is an inseparable sharing between speaker and listener.

THE MESSAGE

Let us look first at the component that is shared by both the speaker and the audience—the message. Most messages are communicated symbolically through a language that is common to the culture. But in using symbolic language we must remember one important principle: The word is not the thing itself; the word is an abstraction of the thing. If listeners have had no experience of the thing the word represents, the word will have no meaning for them. Even if they have experienced it, however, the precise meaning each attaches to the word will reflect his or her own individual experience. Since each person perceives the world from a slightly different angle, a word can rarely have exactly the same meaning for any two people. Of course there must be some common frame of reference, or people would be unable to communicate at all. However, the extent to which a word has the same meaning for two different people is only the extent to which the experiences they associate with it are similar.

In many cases people will believe that they have understood the intended meaning of a word because they have a clear picture of what it means to them. This is particularly true of words that represent abstract concepts. Look at the abstract words in these lines from the Declaration of Independence:

> We hold these Truths to be self-evident, that all Men are created equal; that they are endowed by their Creator with certain unalienable Rights; that among these are Life, Liberty, and the Pursuit of Happiness.

Consider the abstract words used in the Constitution to describe the grounds for impeaching a president. The President must be guilty of "high crimes and misdemeanors." What do these words mean? The debate in the House Judiciary Committee in July 1974 showed that the words had one meaning for some members of Congress and a much different meaning for others. How high do the crimes have to be before they warrant impeachment? There is no way to express such concepts except in words. But do the words really convey precise meanings? Listeners will understand the words readily enough, but the meaning each person attaches to them may be quite different from the meaning the speaker intended. This brings us to another important principle of semantics. The meaning itself is not in the words; it is only in the minds of those who use the words. Words do not *contain* meaning; they are merely tools by which we attempt to *convey* it. And the more abstract the word, the less actual meaning it conveys.

Words are merely symbols for our own use in describing something, and of course a word has no effect on the thing it describes. Nevertheless, we often respond to words as though they endowed the thing itself with these qualities. We laud an institution that is described as "democratic" and condemn one described as "dictatorial" even though both may function in exactly the same way. We attach arbitrary word labels to things and then behave as though the label we have applied creates an actual difference in the thing to which we have applied it.

THE SPEAKER

The next component of communication is the speaker—the source of the message. A thought or an idea originates in the human brain and then must be *encoded* into some sort of communicable form. That form is usually symbolic and expressed in words that constitute a language. We refer to this as the *primary* message. But people are capable of sending messages in other ways as well, and we call that *nonverbal communication* or, sometimes, *auxiliary messages*. These auxiliary messages consist of gestures, vocal inflections, facial expressions, postures, and even clothes worn. We know that the way people dress, the way they stand, the way they smile, and the way they project their voices all have an effect upon the primary message. However, the meaning speakers intend to convey is often affected by secondary messages which they did not intend and of which they may not be aware. They may have mannerisms that affect the audience's interpretation of what is said. Their physical characteristics may influence their messages in ways they have not considered. The same words spoken by a black speaker, or an attractive woman, or an elderly foreigner may have entirely different meanings to the audience. The speaker may have an advance reputation that causes the audience to attach a different significance to the words. All these factors influence the message the speaker actually conveys.

THE AUDIENCE

At the receiving end the message must be *decoded*—that is, the listeners must translate what has been seen and heard into some sort of understandable meaning. We know, of course that the same message, delivered by the same speaker, will not necessarily be interpreted the same way by different audiences. Their own backgrounds, attitudes, and beliefs will affect the message they receive. An audience may have strong religious or political convictions that provide them with a completely different frame of reference. Even such subtle factors as the time of day and the atmosphere of the occasion will have an effect. A tired audience may be impatient with jokes, whereas an audience in a frivolous mood may see almost anything as funny. Moreover, each person in the audience will have a slightly different interpretation of the words, and the response of each will be to the message as each interprets it. You can imagine the complexities in a large, heterogeneous audience, and you may wonder how it's possible for a speaker to be understood at all.

WHY STUDY PUBLIC SPEAKING?

You may be thinking to yourself right now, "But I'm not going to run for office; when will I ever have to stand behind a lectern and give formal speeches?" You may not. However, unless you end up living by yourself in a cave, you will be involved in some kind of communication situation about 70 percent of your waking hours. Most of it will be informal conversation, but much of it will be asking questions, reporting on something you have done, being interviewed, making requests to your employer, explaining things to your supervisor, discussing your ideas at meetings, and expressing your feelings to someone who is close to you. These situations require that you be clear and explicit, aware of your own feelings, and sensitive to the responses of your listeners. All these qualities are examined and practiced in a speech course. Let's look at some of the specific things you can expect from this kind of course.

LEARNING TO SAY WHAT YOU MEAN

The first thing a speech course will teach you is how to **organize** your ideas and your information so that you have something to say. You aren't here to learn how to fill the air with meaningless sounds, so don't expect to get by on your "gift of gab." You will also learn how to say what you have to say clearly and succinctly, and in such a way that others will be interested in hearing it. As you have seen, your words are just one component of your message. You will learn specific skills and techniques for delivering it effectively and persuasively. Don't expect a speech course to teach you how to imitate someone else's dramatic style. Each person is different, and therefore each speaker is different. In this course you will learn to develop a speaking style that is uniquely your own.

DEVELOPING SELF-CONFIDENCE

Fear is nature's way of protecting you against getting into serious trouble, and it's a perfectly normal reaction to an unfamiliar situation. When the situation is no longer unfamiliar and you have gained some assurance of your ability to handle it, you lose your fear and begin to enjoy it. All too often people who are well informed and have excellent ideas remain silent simply because they aren't sure how to verbalize those ideas or lack the confidence to speak up. This is frustrating for them, but it is also a misfortune for whoever is deprived of what they could have contributed. You will overcome much of your anxiety about speaking to a group of people once you understand the nature of the phenomenon, learn that you are not alone, and have a few successful experiences under your belt.

LEARNING MORE ABOUT YOURSELF

For many students this is the most important reason for taking a speech course. Up to this point you may have gotten very little feedback about the impression you make on other people. You probably know quite a bit about yourself, but primarily from the inside out. You may be surprised to discover that you come across to others as arrogant or sarcastic when you have no wish to convey such attitudes. You may learn other things about yourself as well. You can find out how much you know or do not know about your subject when you try to explain it to others. You may find out that some of the opinions you had simply accepted as truths don't stand up under close examination, and you may even change your opinions about some important matters. At least you will examine them carefully.

LEARNING TO RELATE TO OTHERS

In learning about the listener's role in the communication process you will become more aware of the feelings and attitudes of other people. You will learn to understand others better and thus be better able to relate to them. You will also become a better listener yourself, so that others will be able to relate more easily to you. In many of your classes you might go through the entire semester without even knowing the name of the person sitting next to you. In this class you will not only get to know everyone sitting around you, but you will learn about their backgrounds, their interests and accomplishments, and their attitudes and beliefs. It's not at all unusual for warm friendships to form under these circumstances. In addition to learning about this particular audience, you will learn some interesting things about audiences in general.

WHAT IS A GOOD SPEECH?

There are many areas of learning in which the desired results depend directly on mastery of the necessary skills and techniques. This is not so in public speaking. You could learn all the proper techniques and still not give a successful speech. Even if the speech were successful, there might be no concrete evidence of the results, and if the results were immediately apparent, there might be considerable disagreement about whether they were desirable. This does not mean that there are no standards for determining the quality of a speech. It means that there is more than one criterion by which a speech can be evaluated. There are times when an excellent speech may fail to move an audience; Lincoln's Gettysburg Address wasn't recognized as great until some time after it was delivered. There are also times when an exceedingly charismatic speaker may fire an audience to such enthusiasm that what he or she actually said is not evaluated objectively until many years later.

Generally an audience will respond to a speech on **several** different levels:

Artistic Value　This level includes the skillfulness of your organization, the imaginativeness of your material, your sentence structure and choice of words, and the eloquence of your language.

Intellectual value   This level concerns the content. You would be judged on the significance of your subject, the soundness of your ideas, and the validity of the evidence with which you support them.

Effectiveness of delivery   This level concerns the way in which you communicate your message to the audience. Part of the evaluation would be based on the clarity with which you speak, your use of timing, inflection, and vocal emphasis, the ease of your stance and effectiveness of your gestures, the rapport you establish with your audience, and the extent to which you capture and hold their attention.

Certainly a speech that is enthusiastically received by the audience can't be classified as a failure no matter how it falls short in other areas. Still, it wouldn't be fair for an instructor to grade a speech entirely on this basis. Some mediocre speeches are often applauded because the speakers are popular and well-liked or because the audience agrees heartily with their views. Let's see if we can establish some more objective criteria for the speeches you will be giving in class:

The average speech   To meet the requirements for acceptability your speech should conform to the assignment; deal with a significant topic; follow an acceptable pattern of organization; have a clearly stated thesis; and be delivered extemporaneously.

The above-average speech   For an above-average rating your speech should also contain audience-interest factors; have a thoroughly developed introduction and conclusion; have well-organized areas of development; and be delivered with sincerity, enthusiasm, and good technique.

The superior speech   To be really superior your speech should include all the factors mentioned above. In addition, it should display evidence of thorough research coupled with creative thinking; it should deal with a challenging topic and show intellectual insight into this topic; it should demonstrate a superior ability to handle language; and it should be delivered effectively, with some element of style.

With these criteria in mind we can proceed to examine the message, the speaker, and the audience.

QUESTIONS FOR DISCUSSION

1 Would you agree with Gorgias that people are more likely to be persuaded by the style of delivery than by the content of the speech? Can you think of any speakers who rely more on delivery than on the meaning of their words? To what extent do you feel it is ethical to use style as a means of achieving your end?

2 How would you define rock music to someone who had never heard it?

3 What do the words "truth," "rights," "life," "liberty," and "happiness" mean to you? Give some concrete examples to illustrate your meaning.

4 When someone attaches a meaning to your words that is not the meaning you intended, have you conveyed a message? If so, would you say that the message was the meaning you intended or the meaning the hearer understood?

5 Would you say that a "gift of gab" is an advantage in communicating to others? In what ways might it be a handicap?

6 How can a speaker tell whether a speech has been effective? On what basis do you think a speech can best be evaluated? What would you say was the most important criterion for a good speech?

SUGGESTED ACTIVITIES

1 Make a list of the people in public life you consider to be good speakers. What characteristics contribute to their effectiveness?

2 Write down the slang expressions that are often used by you and your friends; then write standard English phrases that mean the same things. Compare your list with those of others in the class.

2

SELECTING YOUR PURPOSE AND SUBJECT

Public speaking is a mode of oral communication in which one person talks to many, implementing either a planned or a spontaneous structure. It is by no means the most effective mode of communication, because the speaker generally gets little if any assurance from the listeners that they have received the message in the form that was intended. Why then, do college classes continue to use the traditional lecture system? The answer lies in the word "economy." Public speaking, whether as a classroom lecture, a presidential address, or a religious sermon, has one important advantage: It allows one person to share ideas and information with a large group in a short period of time. This is why the art of public speaking has remained the cornerstone of oral communication for three millenniums and why great people have devoted their lives to the study of it. It should be apparent, however, that unless speakers are able to convey their information clearly and succinctly, they lose the one important advantage that public speaking has over other modes of communication.

We say that public speaking is a *structured* communication mode—that is, the progression of ideas form a pattern and move in a logical sequence from the beginning to the end. That which we call a "speech" is a self-contained unit and is designed to stand alone—in contrast to a "conversation" or "group discussion" which is communication *in process.* There is an art to conversation and to group discussion, just as there is to public speaking, but *structured* communication tends to be less time-consuming and allows the speaker to convey more information in a shorter period. No type of communication is superior to any other; each has its advantages and disadvantages, and the best choice depends entirely on the circumstances and the needs of the particular situation. In this book we will be dealing primarily with structured communication.

THE PURPOSE OF YOUR SPEECH

In the eighteenth century the rhetorician George Campbell classified speeches according to the intent or purpose of the speaker. His categories are loosely constructed, but nevertheless useful in terms of looking at the broad spectrum of speech purposes:

The speech to entertain   This is sometimes called an *after-dinner* speech and is designed primarily to amuse the audience. There is no expectation that people will need to remember what has been said. It generally consists of a series of humorous references worked around a central theme, and any real information that may be included would be only incidental. This is the kind of speech you might hear at a victory banquet or at the senior class revue, when the audience is relaxed and in a frivolous mood.

The speech to inform   This may be called an *expository* speech because it is designed to expose information rather than to advocate some particular point of view. The topic should be a noncontroversial one, so that the audience does not become involved in taking issue with the speaker. This is the kind of speech that would be given as a report to a committee, where the speaker's responsibility is not to make a decision, but to provide information so that the committee can make a decision. It is also the kind of speech you would expect to hear in a college lecture hall.

The speech to convince   This is a speech designed to persuade the audience to some point of view to which they may be opposed or apathetic. Both emotional and logical appeals are employed to bring the audience around to the speaker's way of thinking. This is the kind of speech you would hear in a debate, in a courtroom, or in a political campaign.

The speech to motivate   This is a speech designed to move people to action. The purpose is to get people to act upon their beliefs—to contribute money, to support a cause, or to play for a team. It is effective only with an audience that is in basic agreement with the goals of the speaker. It generally is the kind of speech that contains highly emotional language.

When you are in the process of planning your speech you should consider your general purpose, but normally this is not stated directly in the speech. For example, to say, "My purpose is to convince you . . ." or, "My purpose is to motivate you . . ." may create unnecessary resistance to what you intend to do.

Often your general purpose will be selected for you or at least implied by the nature of the situation. If you are involved in school politics, you may be called upon to give a "warm-up" speech at a rally; or to explain to a group of people the procedure for voting; or to debate a controversial issue; or to urge people to campaign for a candidate. In all of these cases there will be a general purpose, but you will find that there is a great deal of overlap. Information, humor, argumentation, and emotional language are frequently elements that are contained in the same speech.

Another factor to consider is that the response of the audience is not always in accord with the intent of the speaker. For example, a speaker may intend only to be informative in discussing the theory of evolution. However, if the audience believes in a fundamentalist interpretation of the Bible, this topic will be, inherently, highly controversial. The speaker wishes to inform, but the audience will respond to the speech as if it were an attempt to persuade them to another point of view. How then should the speech be classified—as informative or persuasive? Most theorists would agree that the response of the audience is paramount: The speech would have to be classified as persuasive if that's the way the message was received. You may think you are "just giving the facts," but your listeners will have their own reactions to the facts you select, regardless of your intended purpose.

THE SUBJECT OF YOUR SPEECH

Let's focus our attention on the two basic speech purposes: *inform* and *convince*. The other two are also important but are highly stylized and may be more appropriately handled in an advanced speech class.

TOPICS FOR THE SPEECH TO INFORM

There are numerous sources to aid you in selecting a topic for the informational speech—books you have read; movies, plays, television shows, courses you have taken. You might think first in terms of your own experiences—trips you have made, places you have lived, hobbies you have had, people you have met. Maybe you have worked as a forest ranger, or collected examples of South American folk music, or lived through a tornado, flood, or earthquake. It's likely that you have a great deal of firsthand knowledge.

Your instructor may ask you to select a topic in your academic field, one that requires library research as well as personal experience in such areas as psychology, sociology, history, government, economics, anthropology, or geology. If so, take advantage of this opportunity to clarify for yourself what you have learned in other courses. You have probably observed that things often become clearer in your own mind when you have to explain them to someone else. You may find in the process that your difficulty in explaining something to another person stems from the fact that you don't really understand it as well as you thought you did. Bear in mind that topics dealing with mathematics and the sciences may be completely mystifying to listeners who have no grounding in the basic principles relating to these areas; you must be prepared to fill in the fundamentals.

There are a few things to keep in mind in selecting the topic of your speech:

It must be significant. Don't waste your time, your instructor's time, and the time of your audience with idle chatter. The right to speak carries with it the responsibility of having something worthwhile to say.

It must be of interest to the audience. You haven't been given the floor to show off your knowledge or reminisce about your past experiences. You are there to meet the needs of the audience, not your own need to speak.

It must be something you are enthusiastic about. The most common reason for the failure of a speech is the speaker's lack of enthusiasm. Pick a topic that will really turn you on. The chances are that it will do the same for the audience.

BRINGING YOUR TOPIC INTO FOCUS

Don't overestimate the amount of material you can cover in the six to eight minutes you will have for your speech. You won't be able to discuss the whole field of coin collecting, but you should be able to discuss certain rare coins from one particular country. Millions of words have been written in the field of psychology; you have time for fewer than a thousand of them, but you might be able to cover the uses for aptitude tests in that length of time. How closely you limit your topic may depend on the depth of your knowledge in that limited area. One student spoke for eight minutes on the operation of one valve on a scuba tank. As a general rule, you should narrow your topic as much as you can without having to pad your speech or repeat yourself.

POSSIBLE AREAS OF DEVELOPMENT

Remember that when you start organizing your material you are going to have to break your topic down into more specific areas of development. After you have picked your topic, ask yourself,

"What are some specific aspects of this topic that I can cover?" In a speech on skydiving, for instance, you might discuss packing the parachute, exiting from the plane, maneuvering in the air, and landing. These subtopics will become your main headings when you begin writing your outline. If you can't think of any subtopics, the chances are that your topic is too limited, and you should try to broaden it. For example, a speech on the use of chopsticks might be expanded to include other oriental eating utensils.

YOUR PURPOSE STATEMENT

The first step in preparing your speech is to write out *one statement* that tells clearly and concisely what your speech is about. Your purpose statement should be tentative until you begin to research your topic and find out whether the information you need is available. There are some general rules for constructing your purpose statement:

It should be a complete sentence, phrased the way you normally speak.   This is approximately the way you are going to say it when you deliver your speech.

It should be a statement, not a question.   You may use a rhetorical question to lead into your purpose statement, but the statement itself should be a declarative sentence.

Phrase it so that it focuses on the audience, not on you.   Remember that this is a college speech class, not "show and tell." If you are going to talk about your trip to Europe, don't begin with

Let me tell you about my recent trip to Europe.

Turn it toward your audience:

When you plan your trip to Europe, think ahead about what you want to see and do, where you want to stay, and how you want to travel.

Here are a few examples of the way the purpose statement would be phrased for a speech to inform. Some of these topics will require considerable research; others may be gleaned from your own experience. One word of caution: Do not select a topic that requires visual aids or conditions you cannot provide. For example, you cannot teach people how to swim unless they are in the water. If you are lecturing to them on dry land, you must confine your subject to something they can realistically experience. These topics may give you ideas for speeches you can give in class:

1 It is easy to prepare for a back-packing trip if you follow a few simple principles: have proper equipment, take only what you need, and prepare for emergencies.

2 Before you purchase expensive skiing equipment, be sure to analyze your abilities and your finances.

3 Origami is an ancient Japanese art and can be practiced at almost any level of complexity.

4 There are many things that can be done with macrame for pleasure and for profit.

5 Enology—the study of wine making—can become quite involved, but it is possible to make good wine in your own home.

6 You can learn a great deal about yourself and your behavior patterns through the use of psychodrama.

7 Computers may not be able to solve social problems, but they can provide the data that will lead to solutions.

8 The laser beam has tremendous potential as a tool for industry and may prove to be the key to nuclear fusion.

9 One of the greatest needs for the future may be the devising of new forms of recreation.

10 People who live in condominiums are developing what may become the new American lifestyle.

11 New occupations are opening up every day, but to fill them requires trained people.

12 The college curriculum is being altered to meet modern needs.

13. Most Americans suffer the effects of inflation but have no idea what causes it. There are a number of different theories.

14 You can have fun at the gambling casinos, but your chances of making money are very limited. The odds favor the house.

15 The impressionist school of art is one of the most popular in Europe and America.

16 Buying a house can be a good investment, but there is much to be considered before making a commitment to home ownership.

17 Rock music is often rejected by the intellectual because it is not understood. Actually, it is more complex than many other musical forms.

18 The Hearst Castle in San Simeon is a marvel of architecture and a hallmark of American aristocracy.

19 The urban renewal program is one way the federal government hopes to save the cities.

20 When interest rates go up, a good place to put your money is in bonds, but there is much more you need to know about investing.

A statement of this kind should be written out on paper when you are planning your speech. You will, of course, elaborate on the statement when you actually deliver the speech, but the words you have written out will provide you with a starting point.

TOPICS FOR THE SPEECH TO CONVINCE

The purpose statement for a speech to convince is often called the *thesis*. As the speaker, you are taking a stand on a controversial issue, and your objective is to get your audience to accept your position. You must be clear in letting others know exactly where you stand. Notice how the thesis statement of the speech to convince differs from the purpose statement of the speech to inform.

1 The federal government should provide a minimum guaranteed income for all citizens.

2 Capital punishment should be prohibited in all states.

3 The rights of an unborn child should be guaranteed by constitutional amendment.

4 All young Americans, both male and female, should give two years of service to their country.

5 Legal protection should be afforded to doctors who practice euthanasia.

6 Sex education should be mandatory in all public schools.

7 Homosexual marriages should be given legal status.

8 Federal legislation should restrict the production of unnecessary gasoline-consuming vehicles.

9 The electoral college system should be abolished and replaced by the popular vote.

10 The national defense budget should be significantly reduced.

11 A constitutional amendment should be enacted to provide for national referendums.

12 The Federal Communications Commission should require broadcasters to accept counteradvertising commercials.

13 States should adopt lotteries to raise revenue for public works.

14 Prostitution should be legalized.

15 The federal government should establish a program of national health insurance.

16 Possession of handguns by private citizens should be prohibited.

17 More atomic power plants should be built to ease the energy shortage.

18 Federal and state prisons should be substantially reformed.

19 States should adopt a program of no-fault automobile insurance.

20 The United States should maintain a policy of noninvolvement in the affairs of foreign countries.

These statements deal with some of the most controversial issues of our time, and you should be able to take a stand on any one of them. Don't play the game that politicians are often guilty of playing by deliberately obscuring your position. If you are opposed to a program, say so. Trying to take a stand on both sides at once may not win you the support of anyone. You can, of course, qualify your position, but that qualification should clearly be part of the thesis. For example, you may be in favor of allowing present nuclear power plants to operate, but oppose the development of new ones. That's an important qualification and needs to be stated. Your position, then, is different from those who support all nuclear power plants, and from those who oppose them all.

Generally the purpose, or thesis, of a speech is stated early in the presentation, but there are some exceptions. You may know, for example, that your audience is going to oppose the position you are taking. In such a case, it may be better to use the *indirect* rather than the *direct* approach. In the beginning of the speech you might say, "Let's consider the advantages and disadvantages of the development of nuclear power plants." The value of this kind of statement is that it does not alienate those in the audience who may already have strong opinions. You may use this technique to get them to listen to you, but before the speech is over it will be necessary for you to tell the audience where you stand.

Constructing your purpose statement is one of the most important steps in preparing your speech. If you have crystallized in one or two carefully thought-out sentences exactly what you plan to discuss, you will have a much better chance of saying what you want to say without confusing yourself or your audience. While you are delivering the speech keep your purpose statement in mind. Doing this will help you stay on the track and not wander off onto irrelevant tangents.

QUESTIONS FOR DISCUSSION

1   If public speaking is not the most effective means of communicating, what is? Should colleges and universities abandon the lecture method altogether and substitute group discussion? How informative are the conversations you have with friends?

2 Is it possible to give an informative speech that contains no element of persuasion? If not, where would you draw the line in classifying a speech as informative?

3 Would you agree that public speaking provides more opportunity for persuasion than group discussion? If so, in what way? When you argue with a friend are you really trying to convince or are you just expounding your views?

SUGGESTED ACTIVITIES

1 Write a statement that you think would exemplify each of the four speech purposes—to entertain, to inform, to convince, to stimulate. It may be original or quoted.

2 List three or more topics upon which you would feel competent to speak. After each one write a purpose sentence. Be sure it is well qualified and says what you want it to say.

3 Read one of the statements out loud in class. Have someone ask you a question about it. From your seat reply to the question. Develop your answer as thoroughly as you can in two minutes or less.

3

GATHERING THE INFORMATION

Once you have selected a topic you can talk about enthusiastically, you will have to consider just what you want to say about it. It isn't difficult to fill up eight minutes with words; it is difficult, however, to present specific and meaningful information in this length of time. If your topic is one that you know a lot about, you probably won't be able to cover everything that you know. You will have to decide which bits of information are the most important and then figure out the best way to discuss them in the length of time you have. This is why a short speech is often more difficult to give than a long one. Woodrow Wilson once told a friend that he didn't have time to prepare a five-minute speech, but he was ready at a moment's notice to speak for an hour.

If your assignment is a speech based on some personal experience, you may not have to do any library research. Frequently, however, you will be asked to support your topic with documented information. The following steps will not only save you time in the long run, but will provide you with a technique that you can use for other research projects.

RESEARCHING YOUR SUBJECT

Get an early start on your research to find out if there really is enough information on the topic you have selected. You might not realize the complexity of a subject until you have begun doing some reading. You may also find that you have to change your thesis if the one you picked is not supportable.

INDEXES TO RESEARCH MATERIAL

Indexes are available to provide you with a quick and effective method of locating information in the library. Here are a few of these basic tools that all college students should know how to use:

The Readers' Guide to Periodical Literature   This index is arranged according to topic, with cross-reference to the various subtopics. It will direct you to information appearing in the more popular periodicals such as *Time, Newsweek, Atlantic, and Harpers.*

The Social Science Index; The Humanities Index   These references used to be combined but are now published in separate volumes. Both are arranged and cross-indexed by topic, and will direct you to more specialized professional journals such as *Political Science Quarterly* and *Journal of Philosophy.*

The New York Times Index   This is an excellent index for current affairs. In most libraries copies of *The New York Times* are available on microfilm.

The Education Index   This index will refer you to professional journals dealing wih various aspects of education.

The Business Index   Again, this index is arranged according to topic and will lead you to articles appearing in business journals.

Psychological Abstracts   This index covers the professional journals in the field of psychology and also gives a brief résumé of each of the articles.

GENERAL REFERENCE WORKS

For general background information on historical or scientific topics your best sources are encyclopedias. You are probably familiar with the *Americana,* the *Britannica,* and *Collier's,* but there are also more specialized works such as the *Encyclopedia of Social Sciences,* the *Encyclopedia of American History,* and the *Encyclopedia of Associations.*

For information about people you can consult *Current Biography, American Biography, Who's Who, Who's Who in America,* and *Who Was Who.* For statistical information look in the *World Almanac, Information Please Almanac, Facts on File,* or *Statistical Abstract of the United States.*

After you have checked all these works, ask the librarian for further help. Your librarian is there to assist you, but will be more willing if you can say that you have already looked in the conventional places.

This may seem like a lot of work, and it is; but nobody said it was going to be easy. If you find that your research takes much time and effort, you are probably going about it in the right way. Perhaps the most rigorous kind of speech preparation is that undertaken for a religious sermon. Theologian Charles L. Allen advises as a rule of thumb that ministers spend "an hour in the study for every minute in the pulpit."[1]

RECORDING WHAT YOU READ

Speech preparation can be time-consuming and still not be productive if you fail to keep track of what you read. The beginning speech student may spend many hours in the library, poring over books and periodicals, and not include any concrete

---

[1] "American Preaching: A Dying Art?" *Time,* Dec. 31, 1979, p. 64.

information when the speech is delivered. You must know what to look for when doing your reseach and how to take notes as you read. First of all, remember to record the *source of your information*. Occasionally in the speech you will want to cite the source as well as the information itself. This is particularly true when there may be some question about the validity of the information. In one speech a student made the claim that the United States exports as much oil as it imports. When questioned afterwards, the student responded merely that he had read that in "one of his references." Certainly in this case the source of the information would be as important as the information itself. When credibility may be in doubt, be sure you have specific backing for what you say.

Citing sources is not something you need to do frequently in the speech but it does have the value of letting the audience know that you have done your "homework," and consequently your own credibility is enhanced. It gives the audience the opportunity to judge for themselves the quality of your information. Recognize that some sources are better than others and that you as a speaker need to be an evaluator of reference materials.

In this role ask yourself the following questions:

1 Is the source reputable? That is, has other information from the same source been found accurate?

2 Does the source have any obvious bias? Is it a publication financed by an organization in support of one side or the other of an issue?

3 Has the source provided the complete information, or have important parts been left out? Have quotations been taken out of context?

4 Has the source given the *most current* information, or have late events superseded some of it?

5 Does the information meet the test of reason? Are there internal contradictions? Does the information contradict something else you know to be true?

6 Do other sources corroborate the information? If so, are these other sources reliable? Are there any reasons why one source would possess facts others do not have?

7   Is the language of the source objective? Does the information contain emotionally loaded terms such as "demagogue" and "tyrant"? Is the source attempting to discredit a person or a cause with diatribe rather than reason?

You will come across many sources of information that are not objective and that do try to weight one side of an issue more heavily than another. Your job as a researcher is to determine if this advocacy is reasonable and justifiable, or if it is an attempt to obscure and deceive. The examples you select from your reading and from your personal experience become the warp and woof of your speech. The information must be interesting enough to hold the listeners' attention and useful enough to be remembered.

DEFINITION OF TERMS

The prime requisite of any speech is that it be *understandable*. The vocabulary that you use must be congruent with that of the audience, and words and terms that you use which are outside of their frame of reference must be explained and defined. As you read, make special note of teminology that might be misunderstood or not easily recognized.

Technical words   In a speech on nuclear energy to a lay audience you may have to distinguish between "fission" and "fusion." If your subject deals with computers you might have to explain what is meant by "microprocessor" and "integrated circuit." Those two terms, by the way, like so many other technical terms, have been added to the language only in the past decade.

Words special to a particular field   Many professional and vocational fields have their own unique vocabularies. In broadcasting, for example, the term "combo operator" means a person who functions as both engineer and announcer. That term would have to be explained.

Common words that have specialized meaning   It is possible that the audience will know the meaning of a word, but not understand how it is used in a particular context. The word "viable," for example, might be easily recognized, but not understood as it pertains to abortion. A viable fetus is one that is able to live after it is removed from the uterus.

Words that have taken on new significance   Not only is technology adding new words to the language, but it is reviving older ones. The word "eugenics" has become a significant term as a result of our recent advances in genetic engineering. Eugenics is the study of hereditary improvement.

Words that may be given different definitions   The study of semantics tells us that words are not *containers* of meaning; they are tools we use to convey meaning. We can define a word in any way we want, as long as other people know how we are using that word. Some words, such as "pornography," have to be defined by the courts. Others carry emotional connotations that might have to be clarified. The word "euthanasia" literally means, "good death" but that definition is certainly one that needs further explanation.

Meanings determined by quantitative measure   If you were to say that you favored giving federal aid to people in poverty, you would have to define what you mean by the term "poverty." In this case the definition is continually changing as the cost of living changes. At one time the Council of Economic Advisers defined poverty as the conditions that prevailed when an urban family of four was living on an income of $4,500 per year. In today's economy, of course, that line would be drawn much higher. But you can see how the number of people considered to be in poverty could be modified by raising or lowering the economic definition.

Communication would be much simpler if each word had only one meaning, but such is not the case. Only numbers and some scientific terms have single meanings. Words at a high level of abstraction can be defined in a variety of ways, and for each meaning there are even more connotations. A speaker must spend an appropriate amount of time defining words that may cause confusion. Just what does the speaker who says "I favor *amnesty* for draft evaders" mean? The dictionary defines it as "forgetfulness," but the popular connotation is "forgiveness." It is possible that an entire speech may be a definition. This would be the case if the subject were something like "academic freedom" or "civil disobedience." You as the speaker can define terms the way you want. It is up to the audience to decide if they will accept your definition or not. It may be necessary to use the exclusionary method and tell how you have restricted the meaning. In a speech on euthanasia, for example, you may want to exclude from consideration the active induction of death and talk only about *allowing* someone to die. Without that clarification an objection might arise over a misunderstanding rather than over an issue.

SPECIFIC INSTANCES

When selecting a speech topic you may pick a subject with which you have had direct experience. By doing so you will be able to cite specific instances that come from your own observation or involvement. But the experience of any one individual is limited; consequently you will need to use examples that come from other sources. As you read, look for facts that you find interesting and that can help you put together a generalization about the topic on which you are speaking. You may wish to cite a number of specific instances that contribute to the support of one main idea, or to take one instance and elaborate upon it. Let's look at this example from *U.S. News and World Report,* May 12, 1980, p. 70:

> The high cost of conventional energy has led business to take new approaches or to improve old ones:
> - Recovering methane gas from old sanitary landfills.
> - Producing gas from sawdust.
> - Using a computerized clock thermostat that anticipates heating and cooling needs according to outdoor temperatures.
> - Installing an airfoil that uses the lift force of wind to produce electricity.
> - Devising a vacuum system to dry grain.
> - Employing a trailer-mounted device that crushes cans and bottles at local recycling centers.

In the same article there is one item that receives greater elaboration than the others. It concerns a man who invented a device that cuts fuel consumption in air-conditioned cars. The article explains that while the device works well, the inventor has had a hard time marketing it. In your speech you might want to give all the important details: the man's name, an explanation of how the device works, how long it took him to develop it, and the problems he had getting it on the market.

The illustrations you select are, of course, subject to your own interpretation. The source from which you get the information will have its own point of view, but that does not need to be the one you adopt in your speech. A list of energy-saving and energy-producing devices might lead you to any one of a number of conclusions: that we need not pursue nuclear energy, or that gas rationing is unnecessary, or that more grant money should be made available.

Specific examples are valuable in a speech because they help to gain and hold the attention and interest of the listener and because they contribute to the main contentions that are advanced. But they are limited in what they are able to accomplish. One instance, or even a series of instances, is generally not sufficient to prove a case. In order to provide a broader base for your supporting evidence, you will need to add some statistical data.

STATISTICAL DATA

The case of the man who had a good idea but had difficulty in marketing his product may be an indication that not enough support is given to independent inventors, but your listeners will probably require corroborating evidence. After all, that one instance might be an exception. To give a larger picture, add statistical data. The same article in *U.S. News and World Report* tells us that "small firms have accounted for one half of U.S. inventions since World War II . . . yet they only receive about four percent of federal research-and-development money." Now with that additional evidence the case you are building begins to take shape.

Statistical data are any kinds of information that can be expressed in numbers. The data may be in the form of totals, percentages, averages, rates, or other numerical values. They can be obtained by actual count or from a random sample; they may be expressed orally or displayed on charts. Most important, they must be accurate, and they must be understandable to the audience.

You can probably find figures to support almost any assertion; make sure the ones you use are both *valid* and *reliable*.

During the 1936 presidential campaign a poll of prospective voters showed that Alf Landon would defeat Franklin D. Roosevelt by a landslide. The outcome, of course, was just the reverse. The *Literary Digest*, which conducted the survey, had selected its sample from the telephone directory and automobile-registration records. However, in 1936, in the depths of the Depression, the only people who had telephones and automobiles were those in the high-income brackets, who tended to be Republicans. Thus the results of the survey were not valid because the sample did not represent the entire voting public. Such surveys may also be unreliable because people don't always end up voting the way they said they were going to.

As with other quotations, the reliance the audience places in your figures will depend in large measure on their regard for the source. The U.S. State Department reports and the official Communist Party records give very different figures for party membership. Both are certainly authoritative sources, but your audience may not view them as equally reliable.

More often it isn't the statistics themselves that are misleading but the conclusions that are drawn from them. Figures that show a rising crime rate may not necessarily indicate an increase in crime; they may merely reflect an increase in arrests. Sometimes they indicate a greater willingness on the part of the public to file complaints. Rape cases, for example, were less likely to be reported in the past than they are now. The records show that more automobile accidents are caused by men than by women. However, this doesn't mean that women are better drivers; it just means that men do more driving. Recognizing such fallacies in the use of statistics is not just the responsibility of the audience. It is also the responsibility of the ethical speaker.

The advantage of statistics is that they give to the listener the "big picture" and add significance to your assertions. The danger is that statistics can be carelessly used. Numbers can be manipulated by words as illustrated in the following example:

> *Three men decided to share a hotel room that cost $30. They each paid the clerk $10, and went up to the room. Later, the clerk remembered that the room had been reduced in price to $25, so he told the bell-hop to take five dollars back to the three men. On the way up to the room the bell-hop decided to keep two dollars for a tip. He gave the men three dollars, so they*

> *each got a dollar back. The room then cost each man*
> *nine dollars instead of ten. Three times nine is 27; the*
> *bell-hop kept two. What happened to the other dollar?*

In this example the arithmetic is accurate, but the words used to relate the story are deceptive. The same can be true when statistical information is used in a speech. *Figures do not speak for themselves.* The speaker has an obligation to interpret the figures in a responsible way so that they clarify an issue rather than obscure it.

The emphasis you place upon the statistical data and the way you state the evidence will have a lot to do with the impact the numbers have upon the listeners. For example, it may true that a corporation's profit increased 100 percent. But it could also be true that its profits went from 2 to 4 percent. Both of those statements might be perfectly accurate; the speaker has the prerogative of selecting which one to use.

There are certain extrapolations you can make from statistical data. If a survey indicates that 54 percent of the eligible voters cast a ballot, you can assume that 46 percent did not. But there are precautions you must take in making assumptions. The Bureau of the Census reported that in the past decade the number of marriages per 1000 population remained the same, but the number of divorces doubled. The ratio of marriages to divorce in this country is now about two to one. That evidence does not mean, however, that one out of two marriages will end in divorce, because many people get married and divorced more than once. What's more, it is not a reasonable extrapolation to say that any particular couple has a 50 percent chance of getting a divorce. Statistics, no matter how accurate they may be, are not able to predict individual behavior.

Statistical data can often become confusing unless they are expressed clearly by the speaker. One way to do this is to provide an illustration that the listener can visualize. Consider this example that appeared in *Harpers*, October 1979, p. 28:

> *If you took all the liquid petroleum produced from all*
> *the wells drilled on earth since the first, at Titusville,*
> *Pennsylvania, in 1859, and poured it into a lake the size*
> *of Chicago, roughly 227 square miles, the 330 billion*
> *barrels the earth has yielded so far would fill the lake*
> *to a depth of only 300 feet. The estimated petroleum,*

worldwide, that could be recovered at current prices and technology would fill the lake to a depth of 2,300 feet.

Information presented in this fashion is graphic and therefore more apt to be remembered than if the figures alone were given. Remember, though, that it is an estimate and not an actual count; that may make the information suspect. In this case, citing the source of your information may be important in establishing credibility.

TESTIMONIAL EVIDENCE

Much of the evidence you will want to include in your speech will not be quantitative and will need to be expressed in words rather than numbers. Again, you will want to go beyond your own experience and relate observations that have been made by other people. This type of support is called *testimonial evidence* and can be divided into several categories.

Eyewitness accounts   Court trials rely heavily upon this type of testimony. Witnesses will be called to describe in detail precisely what they saw or heard. They must testify only to that which they actually experienced—what other people told them is called "hearsay" evidence and is not admissible. While eye-witness accounts are given great weight by judges and juries, such testimony is not infallible. Many experiments have been conducted showing that wide discrepancies can appear in the accounts of different witnesses to the same event. When there are several eyewitnesses who all testify to having seen the same thing, the evidence is very strong. But if one person saw something that no one else did, the evidence may be open to some question. Often cases of "flying saucers" are regarded with skepticism when viewed by only one observer, so a speaker relating such an event will need to offer more than the testimony of just one person.

Expert testimony   Often courts will call to the stand people who are referred to as *expert witnesses*. These are people who have expertise in a particular field and are able to verify the results of a study, experiment, or observation. They are able to understand technical data and relate scientific findings that are pertinent to the case. A ballistics expert, for example, can testify that two bullets were fired from the same gun. The listener does not need to understand the technology of such a finding, only that an expert has testified to that effect. For a speaker gathering information, expert testimony is valuable because it is succinct. If the source of the data is credible, there is no need to present the details.

Projections   There is a difference between reporting on what has happened or what has been observed and making a projection as to what *will* happen. No one can foresee the future, of course, and yet we have to make decisions based upon our expectations of what will occur. We put our confidence in those who seem to be in a position to make the most accurate predictions. The people you quote do not have to be well-known personalities so long as they are acknowledged authorities in the subject area in question. Be sure to cite the name and the credentials of the person you are quoting. If you were giving a speech on the deregulation of airline fares, for example, you might quote Richard J. Ferris, President of United Airlines. In *Business Week,* November 5, 1979, p. 105, he said, "There's no question about it. Prices will go up as we said they would. But they will go up less fast than they normally would because the competitive system is much more effective than the government system of regulating prices. . . ." This is an opinion, and, of course, one that could be stated by anybody. But the fact that it is the opinion of the president of a prominent airline company makes it worth quoting. In weighting the information, however, consider the bias of the person who is quoted and the possibility that there are other airline executives, equally prominent, who might disagree.

EXPLANATION

Much of what you will be doing in both the speech to inform and the speech to convince will be providing explanation. As the speaker, you must be sure you understand the material thoroughly yourself. You may look at explanations a number of different ways.

Analysis   To get a complete picture of a concept or a process it is necessary to take it apart and examine it piece by piece. This is what we mean by the term *analysis.* Explanation can be provided for an audience by pointing out the elements that need to be understood. Writing in the December 1, 1979, issue of *The New Republic,* Carl Goldstein, Assistant Vice President of the Atomic Industrial Forum, explains a consideration of solar energy. He says it is clean in the same sense that electricity is clean—at the point of consumption. But he explains that large quantities of copper ore must be mined to meet the needs of solar converters. And, he says, "... the tails left by this mining operation are significantly more radioactive than uranium tails themselves." This line of analysis can be paraphrased in your speech, but credit should be given to Mr. Goldstein for having raised the point.

Historical background   While you are doing your research try to think of what information your audience will need in order to understand the point you are trying to make. Some audiences require more historical background than others, so it may be wise to make note of names and dates and places that may provide helpful orientation. Even if you decide not to use the information in the speech, you should have it in your head in case questions are raised by the audience. If you are giving a speech on abortion, for example, you should know that the decision which guaranteed the right of all women in this country to obtain an abortion was made by the Supreme Court on January 22, 1973, in the case of *Roe vs. Wade.* The details not only give the audience valuable information, but establish you as being a person who is knowledgeable on the subject.

Description   Another form of explanation is description. If you have the ability to paint word-pictures, you can create images in the minds of your listeners. You may want to describe what it is like living in an urban slum; or you might wish to describe the beauty of Yellowstone National Park. This form of rhetorical development can be extremely effective if you are skillful in selecting relevant details and using vivid language. Description can be a powerful persuasive device if employed for that purpose. Again, using the speech on abortion as an example, you could sway your audience one way or the other by your description of the abortion procedure.

Narration   Closely related to description is a method of development called *narration.* When you tell a story, you create suspense, and suspense is effective in gaining and holding attention. Consider this example that appeared in the January 5, 1980, issue of *The Nation*. Fred Powledge writes:

> *I took my daughter's bright yellow hair dryer apart carefully, laying all the parts out in order. There was a possibility I wouldn't find what I was looking for, and I might have to put it back together right away. The bright red one that my wife uses had been O.K. But when I got my first glimpse of the entrails of Polly's dryer . . . I shuddered involuntarily, the way I have reacted upon seeing a rattlesnake in the woods. Inside the bright yellow plastic machine, the one I had bought my daughter less than a year ago, was a short, thin-walled cylinder of asbestos, a poison far more terrifying than rattlesnake venom.*

Narration of this kind might come from your own experience, but you can recreate it by using material from sources. Again, remember that if you use it word for word, or substantially as it was written, you must give the author credit.

Analogy   An effective aid to explanation is analogy. Most people can learn better when new information is compared to something that is already understandable to them. If you wanted to explain the flow of electricity through a wire, you might compare the concept to the flow of water through a pipe. In a speech on this subject you could say that the water's motion is called the *current*, the pressure that pushes the water is the *voltage*, the valve that controls the flow is the *resistance*, and the work done by the water is the *power*. With this picture in mind, the listener might better be able to understand your explanation.

In addition to simplifying complex material, analogies can also be used to add color and vividness to language. In doing this, the points you make in the speech and the ideas you advance are more likely to be remembered. In a speech on career planning you may want to make the point that sometimes it is necessary to move on to a new occupation, even though there may be some risk in doing so. Your analogy could be to that of a circus aerialist who must let go of one trapeze and spend an agonizing second in midair without any support before grabbing on to the next bar. Having established the analogy, the speaker can, for dramatic impact, make reference to it again later in the speech.

Analogies can be used in comparing two institutions. Suppose someone suggested that the United States should adopt a program of compulsory health insurance because it is just as important to provide every citizen with good health as with a good education. This person might argue that since an educated populace is essential to a strong democracy and many would not go to school unless the law demanded it, we have compulsory education and free public schools. Since it is just as necessary for the citizens of a democracy to be in good health, we should also provide free medical care.

Analogies need not be short. They can be extended and, in fact, encompass the entire speech. An analogy of the current period in United States history to that of the Roman Empire during the reign of Nero might be made to emphasize the need for a change in our social mores. In drawing such an analogy, there would be numerous opportunities for comparison—the exploitation of foreign lands, mastery in building, bread and circuses, corruption in government, sexual freedom, etc. In such a speech there would be possibilities for providing information not only about our own country, but also about the Roman Empire. Analogies can be found in the research you do, or they can be invented. They can add considerable color and impact to a speech, but like any of the other means of support we have discussed, they should not be relied upon completely as the sole means of development.

FACTORS OF INTEREST

In either the speech to inform or the speech to convince, it is necessary for the speaker to hold the listeners' attention. In doing your research make sure you look for factors of interest—examples that are not only informative, but will make the audience want to listen. Here are a few ideas along those lines:

Humor   This is one of the most effective means of establishing rapport with the audience. When you get the audience to laugh, they are actively participating in the communication process. To do this, you don't have to be a comedian, and you don't have to feel that you need to be funny all the way through the speech. But humorous reference will do a lot toward gaining attention.

Incidentally, if you tell a joke, be sure there is a point to it that is relevant to the speech. Even if the joke does not get a laugh, you can still make the point.

Suspense   Since the tales of Scheherazade, suspense has been used as a device to pique listeners' interest and hold their attention right through to the end. The example of narration in this chapter gives you an idea of how to tell a suspenseful story.

Uniqueness   Unique examples can be like spices in a stew. You can't rely upon them totally because there are other things you have to include, but they can certainly enhance the flavor of a dish that might otherwise be bland. One unique example that a student included in a speech was the study showing that a flatworm could be conditioned more easily after it had been fed another flatworm which had already been conditioned. The speaker suggested that perhaps students could learn more easily if the instructor were carved up and served to the class.

Familiar references   Have you ever been daydreaming during a lecture and then snapped back to attention when the speaker mentioned the name of a friend, or a place you had visited, or an incident you were involved in? This is a phenomenon that good speakers recognize and use as an effective interest factor. It's not always possible for you to know what references will be familiar to your audience, but you can make some good guesses. To start with, you can use references to other speeches that have been made in class, characteristics of your instructor or other students, or local places and events. Allusions to television commercials, for example, never fail to get an audience reaction.

Vital statements   People generally pay attention to things that are going to affect them directly. This is why newspapers often devote more space to local news than to world events. A discussion of inflation in terms of the gross national product or the cost-of-living index won't arouse your audience as much as the effect inflation has upon the products they buy. When you begin talking about increases in the cost of hamburgers or gasoline, you will start to get their attention.

Bear in mind that people can listen faster than you can talk. Studies have shown that the normal attention span is only a matter of seconds. This means you will not only have to capture the attention of your audience, you will have to keep on recapturing it every few seconds. No one is going to compel your audience to listen to you. Their attention will depend entirely on what you say and how you say it.

BIBLIOGRAPHY

After you have finished your research you should be able to write out a fairly substantial bibliography of sources you have used. This is a valuable thing for you to do even if it is not required by the instructor. Having a bibliography means you can go back to your sources for additional information if that becomes necessary. It also means you can tell your listeners where your information came from. Keep in mind that a bibliography must contain all the data necessary for anyone to retrieve the material quickly and easily. A bibliography of references used in this chapter would look like this:

"Airlines Hit a Downdraft" *Business Week,* Nov. 5, 1979, p. 105.
"American Preaching: A Dying Art?" *Time,* Dec. 31, 1979, p. 64.
Goldstein, Carl, "Clouds over Solar Energy," *The New Republic,* Dec. 1, 1979, p. 8.
"No Shortage of Ideas to Solve the Energy Crisis," *U.S. News and World Report,* May 12, 1980, p. 70.
"Oil in Abundance," *Harpers,* Oct. 1979, p. 28.
Powledge, Fred, "The Asbestos Pistol," *The Nation,* Jan. 5, 1980, p. 14.

Thorough and effective research is the foundation of good speech making. Your ability to identify and select interesting and informative examples is certainly the most important factor in determining the quality of your speech. Here are a few general guidelines to follow after you have done the reading:

Vary your methods of support. Just as a speech containing only statistical examples would be dull, so would one that relied entirely on quotations, or entirely on definitions. Be sure that you have different kinds of supporting material.

Be selective. In the six to eight minutes you have for your speech you won't be able to give a long dissertation. You will have to limit yourself as to examples, so be sure you pick the best ones. This doesn't mean you should stop collecting information as soon as you have eight minutes' worth. Gather all the information you can, and save the excess for any discussion that might come up afterward.

Always use more than one source. You may be tempted to base your speech on some particular article that you have found interesting. Even if you put the material in your own words, basing your speech on someone else's work is still plagiarism. Aside from the ethics of such a practice, it is technically illegal.

Be prepared to change your thesis if necessary. The success of your speech will depend to a large extent on the interest you create with your examples. Don't blind yourself to interesting material just because you have already decided on your thesis. In the course of your research you may come across an excellent item that is relevant but doesn't quite fit in. You may be able to reorient your thesis so that you can use it. Sometimes, in fact, it isn't a bad idea to reverse the usual procedure and develop your thesis after you have seen what information is available.

QUESTIONS FOR DISCUSSION

1 Would you say that one person's opinion is just as good as another's? If not, what is it that makes a difference?

2 There's an old saying that "figures never lie, but liars sure can figure." In what ways can figures and statistics be misleading? Can you give some examples?

3 Are you more inclined to believe a statement when it is made with confidence and assurance? When you hear two conflicting statements, how do you decide which is true?

4 What is it that makes some speeches interesting and others dull? Can you think of other interest factors besides the ones mentioned in the text?

5 Does the attention of the audience depend entirely on what is said and how it is said? What are some things that might interfere with audience attention?

SUGGESTED ACTIVITIES

1 Copy an entry from the *Readers' Guide to Periodical Literature.* Write out fully all the abbreviations.

2 Select a magazine in a subject area that interests you. From the titles of the articles list the possible speech topics you think could be developed.

3 Find a specific fact from your publication. Using your own words, write an assertion that would precede it. Be prepared to state the source of your fact.

4 Find an example of each of the methods of supporting an assertion—definiton, quotation, specific case, statistic.

5 As an oral exercise develop an assertion by means of a short, simple narration.

4

ORGANIZING YOUR MATERIAL

Now that you have gathered the information, your next step is to reflect upon it. What does it all mean? What conclusions can you draw from it? How are you going to put it together? It has to make sense to you before it will make sense to anyone else. You need to consider whether the material lends itself to an informative speech or a persuasive speech. Is the subject matter controversial, and do you wish to take one side of the issue? You can, of course, present both sides and let the audience draw their own conclusions. If the information is noncontroversial, you have the makings of a speech to inform, and since that type is a little less complex than the speech to convince, let's begin there.

GETTING ORGANIZED

If you want to get something done, ask the busiest person you know to do it. Somehow the student who is a member of the college council, president of the debating club, chairman of the finance committee, and out for track is always the one who can find time for another project. Such people can pack more into a day because they have learned to organize their time. By the same token, some people can pack more information into their speeches than others. The one who speaks the longest is not necessarily the one who says the most. Much material can be presented in a short time if it is clearly stated and properly organized. Good organization is essential to effective speaking for three reasons: it will allow you to say the most in the time that you have; it will permit your audience to follow you more easily and retain what you say; and it will minimize the risk of forgetting what you plan to cover. Being armed with a definite sequence of ideas may also ease the stage fright that arises from fear of forgetting something.

An outline is the most effective means of organizing your material. Once you learn to outline well, you will find it easier and more useful than writing out a complete script because the structure of your speech will be apparent at a glance. Before you begin, make a careful, objective evaluation of all your material. Does it support a central idea? Is it concrete and significant? Will your audience be interested in it? If you get a "no" answer to any of these questions, start over.

PREPARING YOUR ROUGH DRAFT

Your outline must be legible, so plan from the beginning to copy it over. Don't expect to get all your ideas and information down on paper in a neat, well-organized fashion the first time. You will have to cross things out, change headings, and add notations in the margin—at least you will if you are at all concerned about what you are doing. If you plan from the outset on starting with a rough draft and then recopying it, you will be less reluctant to make the necessary improvements on your first effort.

REWRITE YOUR PURPOSE STATEMENT

You wrote your purpose statement before you began your research, but remember that it was only tentative. Look back over Chapter 2 and then write your purpose statement in more or less final form. Make sure it is clearly stated and fully *qualified*. Don't be afraid to use enough words to say what you mean. It isn't enough to say

> *Today I would like to talk about coin collecting.*

This statement is not qualified; that is, it places no restrictions on the vast area of coin collecting. You might improve on it by saying

> *Coin collecting is not only a fascinating hobby, but it can also be a profitable one.*

Now you have introduced your subject, conveyed your attitude toward it, and suggested at least one point of development—profitability.

ADD A PRESUMMARY TO YOUR PURPOSE STATEMENT

The presummary lets the audience know what they can expect to hear. It also provides an opportunity for you to review what you intend to say. If you begin by telling the audience what you are going to tell them, you are less likely to leave out material you had planned to include.

Suppose your purpose sentence was

> *Learning to play the guitar is not as difficult as you may think.*

This states your topic and expresses your attitude toward it, but it doesn't tell your audience much about what you are going to cover. It would be better to add another sentence:

> *To get off to a good start there are two things you need to know—how to select a guitar and how to select a teacher.*

This gives the audience a clue to your organizational pattern and tells them what they can expect in your speech. The presummary becomes part of your purpose statement, but it need not be written word for word on your outline. It would probably look something like this:

> *Learning to play the guitar is not as difficult as you may think.*
> **A** Selecting a guitar
> **B** Selecting a teacher

WRITE YOUR MAIN HEADINGS

The main headings constitute the foundation of your outline. These are the broad generalizations or assertions that your specific examples are intended to support. Write them in complete sentences in the language you normally use when you speak. You don't have to memorize them. Once you have written them out in full-sentence form on your outline, they will come back to you with more familiarity when you deliver the speech.

Your main headings should be consistent with what you said in the presummary, and in the same order.   In other words, follow the pattern of organization you said you were going to use. In the speech on the guitar, for example, your main headings might be in this form:

> **I**   The best guitar for you is not necessarily the most expensive one.
> **II** Before you spend any money on lessons, find out the qualifications of the teacher.

You will confuse your audience if you reverse the order or if you include areas that were not referred to in your presummary.

Your main headings should say something meaningful about your topic.   The audience is more likely to remember the main ideas of a speech than the specific details; be sure that your main point is clear. Instead of saying

> *I'm going to give you some statistics about unemployment.*

it would be better to say

> *The rate of unemployment has continued to increase over the past year.*

Your main headings should follow some pattern.   The particular pattern that is best for your speech depends on your purpose
and the effect you want to achieve. No matter which arrangement
you select, however, be sure that all your headings follow the
same pattern. Don't confuse your audience and yourself by
starting out on one basis and then switching to another.

There are several heading patterns with which you should
be familiar. Consider them carefully, and then decide which
arrangement best suits your needs.

The topical pattern   This is the most common arrangement; it consists merely of breaking the speech down into its
component parts, as we did with the speech on the guitar. Here
is another example:

    I   The legislative branch of our government makes the
       law.

   II   The judicial branch interprets the law.

  III   The executive branch carries out the law.

The chronological pattern   This is a good arrangement
for explaining a process or for discussing some progression:

    I   The first step in constructing a patio is to make your
       forms.

   II   The next step is to pour the concrete.

  III   The final step is to smooth the surface.

The spatial pattern   Some topics can best be discussed in
terms of physical areas. For example, recreational facilities might
be organized according to geographic area:

    I   The coast region offers swimming, surfing, and deep-sea
       fishing.

   II   The mountain areas offer skiing in the winter and back-
       packing in the summer.

They might also be discussed in terms of different levels of
altitude.

The problem-solution pattern   This type of arrangement
might be used for a speech to convince, where the speaker
describes a problem and then shows a solution for it:

    I   Polluted air is not just a nuisance; it's a killer.

   II   One of the major contributing causes is the automobile.

III   The only way to end the smog problem is to eliminate the internal-combustion engine.

The indirect pattern   This pattern would be used where a hostile audience must be persuaded to accept the speaker's viewpoint. The speaker begins with the point that is easiest for them to accept and then progresses to the controversial point of his thesis:

I   The federal government in a democracy has a responsibility for the well-being of the citizens it represents.
II   Many of those people who are in a condition of poverty are there for reasons beyond their control.
III   The federal government should provide a minimum guaranteed income for all citizens.

SUPPORT AND DEVELOP YOUR MAIN HEADINGS

Main headings cannot stand alone. Since they are merely assertions, you have to support them by specific examples. No matter what types of support material you use, the important thing to remember is that the examples must be relevant to the main heading. By the same token, the main heading must clearly govern all the information under it. At times you may have to reword your main heading so that it covers all the examples you want to include, or perhaps narrow it down so that it relates more specifically to the examples you do have.

When you write your outline, number your main headings. Then, when you add your support material, letter each point and indent it under the main heading that governs it. If you have further subpoints, these should also be numbered or lettered and indented under the statement they are intended to support:

I   One of the animals that is becoming extinct is the polar bear.
  A   Josef Van De Brugge: immense numbers in 1670
    1   Estimated 250,000
    2   Seen as far south as middle Canada
  B   Steady decline in population since eighteenth century
    1   William Barents: 1000 seen slain in 1830
    2   125 per month killed by one hunter
    3   Population now about 12,000
      a   Only 50 seen by Eskimos in a lifetime
      b   Will be extinct by year 2000

WRITE YOUR CONCLUSION

Studies show that your conclusion is more likely to be remembered than what you have said in the body of your speech. Utilize this important portion of the speech to its best advantage. If you have held your audience, they will be with you at this point. If you haven't, they will at least be listening for signs that you are about to finish. One way or the other, however, this is the point at which you will have their attention, so make the most of it. If your purpose is to convince your audience or to stimulate them to action, your conclusion might be planned to win them over. Think of some of the famous concluding lines:

> Give me liberty or give me death.
> You shall not crucify mankind upon a cross of gold.

In any speech your conclusion should focus attention on your main idea. You should still be talking at the end of your speech about what you said in your purpose statement. Let's look at some of the methods you might use:

The summary   One of the most common ways of concluding a speech is to summarize your main idea. This might simply be a restatement of your thesis. If it has been a long speech with many complicated points, you may want to reiterate each of the important ones. Your summary should be long enough to make your point, but be careful not to drag it out so that it loses its punch.

The quotation   This can be an effective method of concluding a speech if the quotation is well-phrased and apt. You might get some ideas from *Bartlett's Familiar Quotations,* which is indexed according to subject and author.

The illustrative anecdote   This can be effective as a conclusion if you are a good storyteller. The same factors apply as for narration. Make sure any anecdote you use is to the point and that you are able to tell it clearly and succinctly.

However you decide to end your speech, make sure you have planned it. Don't expect a good conclusion just to happen. Usually it doesn't—and there you are with nothing more to say and no exit line. Plan your exit line, so that you wind up on a strong, dynamic note.

WRITE YOUR INTRODUCTION

If your conclusion is important, your introduction is even more important. The introduction to a speech has several specific functions:

It should orient the audience to your topic.   Let your audience know exactly what you are going to tell them. Be careful not to mislead them by including irrelevant material in your introduction.

It should establish the importance of your topic.   The importance of your topic may or may not be self-evident. Accident prevention in the home, for example, may not seem too significant until you point out that household accidents cause more deaths each year than automobile and airplane accidents combined.

It should establish rapport with your audience.   It is often true that people are not only more willing to accept what you say, but also more willing to believe you if they like you as a person. In those first few seconds your audience is sizing you up, so make the best impression you can. If you want your audience to like you, let them know that you like them.

It should capture the attention of your audience.   Before you can tell your audience anything, they have to be listening to you, and they aren't going to listen unless you have their attention.
    Since capturing the attention of your audience is the most important function of your introduction, let's consider a few specific techniques:

The rhetorical question   A rhetorical question is one designed to plant an idea for consideration. You might begin by saying:

What are the problems that are of most concern to the adolescents of today?

You would then go on to answer this question in the body of your speech.

The startling statement   This can be an extremely effective attention-getting device. An audience is bound to take some notice of the speaker who begins by saying:

It is almost certain that some time within the next ten years California will experience a major earthquake.

The illustrative anecdote   This device can be used just as effectively in an introduction as in a conclusion. Make sure you tell the story well; be clear and succinct. Write out the first few words to be sure you get off to a good start. Even if you think you know the story well, getting started may be more difficult than you realized.

The humorous anecdote   This technique has some advantages as an opener because it not only gains attention, but it also establishes rapport with the audience. If you can get your audience to laugh, you know they are participating in the communication process, and therefore that they are listening. The added advantage is that when the audience relaxes, you are more likely to relax. Make sure, however, that your joke has a point that relates in some way to the main idea of your speech; then, even if you don't get a laugh, you still have a point. The pitfall, of course, is being corny or trite, but be careful, too, about telling off-color jokes; they are very likely to backfire with the wrong audience.

These are just a few of the devices you might use. With a little imagination you should be able to come up with a lot more. The important thing is that your introduction be planned. Getting started is going to be one of your biggest obstacles. Regardless of the kind of introduction you decide on, write out the first words on your outline. Be sure you know exactly what you are going to say when you face the audience and open your mouth.

PREPARE YOUR BIBLIOGRAPHY

Your outline should contain a list of the references you have used. For the sake of practice, you should put them down in regular bibliographic form.

Book
Kennedy, Eugene, *On Becoming a Counselor,* New
York: Seabury Press, 1977.

Periodical
La Brecque, Mort, "On Making Sounder Judgments,"
Psychology Today, June 1980, p. 33.

For other kinds of works ask your English teacher or your librarian
for the proper bibliographic form.

WRITING YOUR FINAL OUTLINE

There are several things to remember when you draft your
outline in final form:

Divide your outline into parts.   Your outline should have four
parts: the introduction, the purpose statement, the body, and the
conclusion. Clearly identify each of the parts, and leave extra
space between them.

Number or letter all your headings.   Designate your main
headings with roman numerals, your subheadings with capital
letters, and your specific examples with arabic numerals.

Use the proper form of indention.   Indicate each level of
subordination by its proper indention, so that the structure is
clear at a glance.
    The point is that the structure of your outline should clearly
display the relationship of each idea. Your instructor shouldn't
have to spend time trying to figure out how your material is
organized in order to see what you plan to say—and neither
should you.
    Look at the following outline for a speech on hypnosis.
Note the device used in the introduction to gain attention. The
purpose statement says clearly what the speech is about, and the
presummary indicates the areas that will be covered. The main
headings are consistent with the presummary, and the support

material is relevant to each heading. Note also that the conclusion reinforces the main idea of the speech.

HYPNOSIS

INTRODUCTION (attention-getting device)

It is somewhat startling to see a man crush a lighted cigarette against the palm of his hand and not get burned or scarred.

PURPOSE STATEMENT

Hypnosis can be a valuable tool when it is used properly and effectively.

1 Theories of hypnosis.

2 Methods of induction.

3 Ways it can be used.

BODY

    I Many prominent people have experimented with hypnosis and have formulated theories about it.

      A Pavlov believed it was the same as sleep.

        1 Not true. There are many differences.

          a Brain-wave patterns.

          b Subject is aware and remembers.

        2 Some relationship to conditioning.

          a Behavior can become habitual.

          b Subject will rationalize.

      B Freud explained it as emotional rapport or thought transference.

        1 Does not account for self-hypnosis.

        2 Thoughts not transferred. Subject conjures them.

      C Modern theories are more accurate.

        1 Prof. H. Bernheim attributes it to suggestion.

        2 Dr. S. J. Van Pelt calls it superconcentration.

   II Hypnosis can be induced three different ways.

      A Hetero-hypnosis. Induction by someone else.

        1 May use an instrument for concentration.

        2 Puts suggestion in subject's mind.

         B Self-hypnosis. Subject induces condition.

         C Auto-hypnosis. Subject becomes hypnotized accidentally.

            1 Fear.

            2 Steady driving for long periods.

  III Uses for hypnosis stretch the imagination.

         A Used in medicine.

            1 Pain killer.

            2 Retarding side effects.

            3 Preventing psychosomatic illnesses.

               a Ulcers.

               b Migraine headaches.

         B Used in psychotherapy.

            1 Helping patient recall.

            2 Establishing new behavior patterns.

         C Used as a tool for self-improvement.

            1 Stop smoking.

            2 Lose weight.

CONCLUSION

Hypnosis can be used by almost anyone. It is a painless, harmless means of making important changes in your life, and it has tremendous potential.

    No matter how good your material is, you don't have a speech until you have organized your ideas and information into a single clear message to present to your audience. This may be the area of speech preparation that will give you the most difficulty because it also requires that you organize your thinking. You may find when you start outlining that your clear idea of what you want to say is a lot hazier than you thought it was. If your speech isn't clear enough for you to outline, it won't be clear enough for your audience to follow.

QUESTIONS FOR DISCUSSION

    1 How much does the length of a speech affect the attention of the audience? What do you think is the optimum length for an effective speech?

2 Do you find there is some structure in your own conversation? In casual conversation do you ever think ahead to what your next point is going to be? Do you ever try to direct a conversation so that it stays on one central idea?

3 What effect does organization have on communication? Is it possible for a speech to be overorganized? If so, in what way might this affect communication?

4 Can you identify the organizational pattern in this chapter? What is the organizational pattern in the next chapter?

5 What techniques besides those mentioned in the text might be used in an introduction? Is it possible for an attention-getting device to be too dramatic? If so, in what way? What might be the result?

SUGGESTED ACTIVITIES

1 Write an introduction and read it to the class. Explain the effect you were attempting to achieve.

2 Interview a student in the class and gather a few salient bits of information about his or her life. Present the student to the class with a short introductory speech. Take a positive attitude, but don't exaggerate the virtues of the person you are introducing.

3 Select a topic that you know something about and write a purpose statement. Add three main headings, each of which you could develop with more detail. Finally, write a summary statement that tells what you have said.

5

FUNDAMENTALS OF PERSUASION

We have looked at the organization of speech to inform; in this chapter we are going to examine the complexities involved in developing the speech to convince. When we say we are going to convince people of something, we mean we are going to try to effect a change in their beliefs, attitudes, or behavior. One way we can do this is by advancing *arguments*. An argument is a rhetorical mode of communication that appeals to an individual's logic or reason. We know that this is an effective means of inducing someone to make a change, but we also know that not all change comes about as a result of appeals to reason. In addition to advancing arguments, the effective speaker will also attempt to reach people at the emotional level. When we refer to the concept of convincing people through appeals to both the intellect and the emotions, we use the word persuasion.

Persuasion is a term that may have negative connotations for some people. It might sound like the art of getting people to do something they do not want to do or believing something they do not want to believe. So let us make some distinctions: Persuasion is not the same thing as *coercion* nor is it the same thing as *manipulation*. Coercion means using force or the threat of force to change behavior. Manipulation implies changing behavior through devious or underhanded methods. Persuasion, in contrast, means effecting a change in beliefs, values, attitudes, or behavior by offering reasons that can be freely accepted or rejected. To use a sexual analogy, coercion could be compared to rape, manipulation compared to seduction, and persuasion compared to making love.[1] Just as all sexual intercourse is not lovemaking, so all change in beliefs, values, attitudes and behavior is not persuasion. As a persuader you are expressing what you honestly believe to be true. You are not trying to take advantage of your listeners—you want them to be the beneficiaries of your message, not the victims. You need to share with your audience the evidence, the reasons, and the logic that you yourself used in arriving at the conclusion you reached. That is why studying public speaking is more than just learning communication skills: In the process you learn to think more clearly about what you consider to be the truth.

We all have our own perception of reality, so truth is what each of us, individually, believes to be true. Since the future is a mystery to all of us, there are gaps in our knowledge. Still, we all must formulate beliefs on the basis of what we know. All of us are subject to persuasion, so our truth is often structured by what someone else tells us. How do we know when to accept something as "true"? What do we regard as being "proof"?

MODES OF PROOF

Aristotle analyzed persuasion in terms of the elements that affect the people to whom the message is directed. He contended that

[1] Douglas Ehninger and Wayne Brockriede, *Decision by Debate,* Harper & Row, New York, 1978, p. 30-31.

those elements or "modes" were the *logos,* the *pathos,* and the *ethos.* These correspond roughly to the argumentation, the emotional appeal, and the character of the speaker.

LOGOS

When we speak of the logos, we are referring to the facts, the evidence, and the reasoning contained in the speech. If a listener's beliefs are based upon information that he or she accepts as true, a speaker might be successful in modifying those beliefs by offering contrary information. The new information must be well-documented and logically presented in order to override the previous beliefs. When persuasion is effected in this way, we say that the speech contains strong *argumentation.* Consider that argumentation is "the study of the logical principles which underlie the examination and presentation of persuasive claims. . . . This definition suggests that the central concern of argumentation is with logical principles. It is this focus on logical processes which distinguishes the study of argumentation from the study of persuasion."[2]

By focusing attention on the evidence, speakers hope to persuade you that their arguments are based entirely on reason. Of course, factual evidence can be found to support either side of a controversial issue; otherwise, by definition, the issue would not be controversial. A speaker merely selects that evidence which supports his or her contention. The information presented may or may not alter the opinion of the audience. They may reject it as untrue or dismiss it as insignificant. They may also consider it insufficient to prove the point. A speaker who contends that a local government is riddled with corruption would need more than one or two examples to make any impression on an audience that supports this government.

PATHOS

The study of psychology tells us, of course, that the beliefs, attitudes, and values that people hold are not always founded upon logic and reason. We know that if a person does not want to change a belief, no amount of information you present is going to make any difference. Clarence Darrow once observed,

---

[2] George W. Ziegelmueller and Charles A. Dause, *Argumentation, Inquiry and Advocacy,* Prentice-Hall, Englewood Cliffs, N.J., 1975, p. 4.

"You don't have to give reasons to the jury. Make them want to acquit your client and they'll find their own reasons."

It is easy to say that we should weigh all the evidence before we make a decision, but we never have all the evidence. There are also times when emotional factors must supersede any objective evidence. The plight of a starving child is not suited to objectivity. The very survival of nations has sometimes been determined by response to an emotional appeal. Franklin D. Roosevelt's appeal to the American people in 1933 was more effective than any factual statement he might have made:

The only thing we have to fear is fear itself.

Appealing to the emotions is a perfectly legitimate means of persuasion as long as the appeal itself is an ethical one.

ETHOS

All through history there have been speakers whose words have swayed millions—Churchill, Hitler, Castro, Kennedy, King. The personal magnetism of such speakers is a quality called *charisma*. But were their words really more potent or more eloquent than words of less magnetic speakers? Can the words themselves be separated from those who spoke them? If someone other than Martin Luther King had said, "I have a dream . . . ," would the words have had the same impact? Ethos, the qualities of character projected by a speaker, is perhaps the most illusive of all the Aristotelian modes of proof. If the audience does not see the speaker as a person who is sincere, trustworthy, and knowledgeable, they may reject the speaker's evidence, and they will certainly reject any emotional appeal he or she may make. Aristotle contended in *The Rhetoric* that a speaker established his ethos directly during a speech:

> *Persuasion is achieved by the speaker's personal character when the speech is spoken as to make us think him credible. We believe good men more fully and more readily than others. This is true generally whatever the question is and absolutely true where exact certainty is impossible and opinions are divided. This kind of persuasion, like the others, should be achieved*

by what the speaker says, not by what people think of his character before he begins to speak.[3]

Nevertheless, it is apparent that when a speaker has a reputation the audience will be influenced by it. They will frequently decide what to believe and what not to believe on the basis of the speaker's prestige. In general people are more inclined to take the word of someone whose opinion is highly regarded by others and whose expertise has received public recognition in the form of rank or position. You may disagree with the Secretary of Defense when he says that the antiballistic missile is necessary to preserve the balance of power, but his opinion is more likely to be taken at face value than yours. Yours will have to be supported.

COGNITIVE DISSONANCE

Regardless of how effective the speaker may be, persuasion can only occur when there is a readiness on the part of the listener to be persuaded. Free choice is an explicit part of persuasion—the receiver of information has the option of accepting or rejecting what is offered. When new information is in conflict with what has previously been believed, people in the audience may summarily dismiss it. But if the assertion is perceived as having some validity, a condition is set up which we call *cognitive dissonance*.[4] This means that an individual's intellectual equilibrium has been upset by a notion that is incongruent with prior thinking. While this condition may not alter a person's belief, it constitutes the first step in the process of persuasion.

Some people avoid having their equilibrium disturbed at all by simply rejecting anything that doesn't fit in with their pattern of thinking. This is the kind of person who might say, "Don't confuse me with facts: my mind is made up." Usually people will consider and evaluate a new idea; however, the extent to which

[3] *The Rhetoric and Poetics of Aristotle*, trans. W. Rhys Roberts, Modern Library, New York, 1954.

[4] L. Festinger, *A Theory of Cognitive Dissonance*, Stanford, Calif., Stanford University Press, 1957.

they are willing to accept it depends primarily on the strength and complexity of their present beliefs. Ideas that touch on strong emotional convictions or are intimately tied to a whole set of values and beliefs are very likely to be rejected regardless of the objective evidence.

To illustrate this theory let us look at the example of a mother who receives information from a reliable source that her teenage son has been taking drugs. If the information is in conflict with what she has previously believed about her son, she may experience the condition of cognitive dissonance. The mother has several choices: She can dismiss the information as being invalid; she can regard the incident as an exception that will not occur again and need not alter her previous beliefs; she can minimize the importance of taking drugs so that it does not jeopardize the image she has of her son; she can allow the dissonance to prevail, not wanting either to change her belief or reject the information; or she can modify the belief she has had about her son and acknowledge that he does have a problem. If she makes the latter choice, we say that persuasion has occurred. Taking that step then allows her to move in the direction of seeking a solution.

As a speaker you have much the same effect when you give information and introduce new ideas. By setting up the condition of cognitive dissonance you create for the listener a need to make a choice. Even if your solution to the problem is rejected, you are successful in your efforts when you are able to convince the audience that a problem exists. You may bring to their attention a social condition about which they had previously been unaware, or you may reopen what might have been a closed issue. From the theory of cognitive dissonance we can conclude that the information you present in your speech is of paramount importance.

PERSUASIVE INFORMATION

In Chapter 3 we discussed methods of research and gathering information. In its raw form, factual information can be employed to develop any kind of a speech, whether the purpose is to inform, to convince, to entertain, or to motivate. The significance of the information you gather is not always self-evident—it can enlighten, persuade, amuse, or inspire, depending upon the way it is used. Information that is intended to be persuasive must be presented in a persuasive framework. The theory of cognitive dissonance suggests that persuasion begins when new information which is regarded as valid is perceived by the listener to be in conflict with previous beliefs. The key factor here is *perception*. The listener must *perceive* two things; that the information is valid, and that it conflicts with previous beliefs. The speaker must facilitate both of these conditions in order for the first step of persuasion to take place. The perceived validity of the information will depend upon the confidence the listener has in the speaker as well as in the source of the speaker's information. The extent to which the information conflicts with previous beliefs depends upon the way the speaker integrates the information into his or her claim.

Giving information is not the same thing as advancing an argument. An argument must contain an assertion, or what you might call a *link* which helps the listener make an *inferential leap* from the previous belief to the new one.

THE INFERENTIAL LEAP

Let's elaborate on the term *inferential leap*. If you were to explain to an audience the newest methods for disposing of nuclear waste, you would simply be providing them information, not advancing an argument. But when you *assert* that these methods are safe, could eliminate leakage, and could be used without creating risk, you are asking the audience to make an *inferential leap* from the known to the unknown. If the assertions you make are confined to those conditions that are verifiable, you are being informative rather than persuasive. In a persuasive message you are calling for the acceptance of an unknown quantity. To illustrate this concept let us combine some of the information we gathered in Chapter 3 concerning small businesses with two different assertions—one informational and one persuasive.

To inform: Small firms have been doing their share in contributing to the country's production. They have accounted for one-half of all U.S. inventions while receiving only 4 percent of federal research-and-development money.

To persuade: The federal government is giving unfair advantages to big business. Small firms receive only 4 percent of federal research-and-development money; yet, they account for half of all U.S. inventions.

In this case we have used statistical information to support the claim. We could also use testimonial information.

To inform: Airline executives generally favor the removal of price controls on air fares. Richard J. Ferris, President of United Airlines, said, "Prices will go up . . . but they will go up less fast than they normally would, because the competitive system is much more effective than the government system of regulating prices . . ."

To persuade: Government price control is not the best way to keep down the cost of air transportation. Richard J. Ferris, President of United Airlines, said, "Prices will go up . . ."

As the presenter of the information you have the responsibility of interpreting your facts in a way that leads the audience to the conclusion you want them to accept.

THE EVIDENCE

The information used to support a speech to persuade is called "evidence." Evidence could, of course, be physical as well as rhetorical, but right now we are primarily concerned with the latter. Rhetorical evidence can be in the form of statistics, testimony, case histories, or any of the other forms we mentioned in Chapter 3. When you propose to lead the audience to a conclusion you want them to accept, your evidence must be presented in a way that will accomplish that end. Extraneous information should be deleted from the speech, and contrary material should be justified in some way. While doing your research you may come across evidence that is contrary to the support of your thesis. When this happens you have three choices: (1) You can leave it out, (2) you can change your thesis, or (3) you can include it, but with refutation. If you include it without refutation, your audience will question the validity of your thesis. Here is an example: A student speaker was advocating that more government support be given to provide housing aid to low income families. She had come across some statistics showing that 94 percent of the population of the United States lived in adequate housing facilities. She included these figures in the speech and then dismissed them by saying they were misleading and did not represent the true picture. But the audience was more impressed by the statistics than they were by her admonition. What can you do when you have to account for this kind of evidence? You might be able to attack the source by contesting the method used in gathering the statistics. You possibly could find other figures that showed a different picture. You could challenge the definition of the term "adequate." But if you were unable to do any of these things you could reconstitute the statistics. Six percent of the population do not have adequate housing. That's over 13 million people—quite a significant number.

The point is that there are a number of interpretations that can be given to any piece of evidence. The speaker's job is to arrange them in a way that makes sense and leads listeners to a reasonable conclusion. In order for that conclusion to be clear in their minds, it must first be clear in yours. The thinking process used to accomplish this is what we call *inductive reasoning.*

INDUCTIVE REASONING

Your reasoning is either *inductive* or *deductive.* When you draw a conclusion from evidence, you are engaging in inductive reasoning; when you apply a belief to a particular case, you are using deductive reasoning. Inductive reasoning is sometimes referred to as *the scientific method.* It begins with a number of examples or observations and proceeds to a conclusion. The validity of the conclusion depends upon the amount and substance of the evidence that supports it. When Newton formulated the law of gravity after observing falling objects, he was using inductive reasoning. Statistical sampling is also done on this basis.

CAUSES

Most of the time inductive reasoning is a matter of simple observation. After you have been in college a while, you learn that if you don't study for an exam you get a low grade. There seems to be a cause-and-effect relationship. Low grades are caused by not studying. But sometimes you get a low grade when you do study. This might happen if the instructor grades on a curve and there are a lot of smart people in the class, or if you have studied the wrong thing. So you learn that other things can cause low grades too. Having arrived at this conclusion, you attempt to control all the variables that might result in a low grade. This is exactly what scientists do; they want to be sure they have correctly identified the actual cause. The weakness in the inductive process is that the evidence may be misleading. What we believe to be causes may in fact have no relationship to the result. A traffic light does not *cause* a car to stop. It causes the motorist to use the foot brake, sometimes. To be sure of not getting hit crossing the street, you may want to wait until the car stops instead of just waiting until the light turns red for it. All too frequently we mistake a *sign* for a *cause*.

SIGNS

A sign is an indication that a thing has occurred or will occur; it is not a cause. When we say, "That man is drunk because he is lying in the gutter," we do not mean that one was the cause of the other. We mean that lying in the gutter is a *sign* of drunkenness. But it could be the sign of something else, too. It might indicate that the man had suffered a heart attack. Signs can be misconstrued and can lead to invalid conclusions.

Both signs and causes are used in the inductive process. The trick is to perceive them accurately. The generalizations that we believe to be true come about as a result of inductive reasoning. Sometimes they are valid; other times they are not. A chauvinistic male may believe that women are careless drivers. Every time he sees a woman make a mistake in traffic his conclusion will be reinforced. He will ignore any evidence that suggests the contrary. Unfortunately such an invalid conclusion will be passed on to another person who will accept it without testing it. Our culture is full of proverbs and aphorisms that people accept and believe with little or no evidence. "Spare the rod and spoil the child" and "A woman's place is in the home" are two examples. Often these beliefs are applied mindlessly.

DEDUCTIVE REASONING

Deductive reasoning is the process of applying the generalization to a specific case. In other words, it is the reverse of inductive reasoning. A parent who has accepted the conclusion that to spare the rod is to spoil the child will administer corporal punishment in a situation where another parent may not; a man who believes that a woman's place is in the home may refuse to allow his wife to get a job regardless of the financial condition of the family. Inductive reasoning and deductive reasoning are both natural processes and can lead to either valid or invalid conclusions.

THE SYLLOGISM

The basis of deductive reasoning is the *categorical syllogism*. A syllogism consists of three statements—the major premise, the minor premise, and the conclusion that follows from them:

> *All men are mortal.*
> *John is a man.*
> *Therefore John is mortal.*

If both premises of a valid syllogism are accepted as true, then, according to the laws of formal logic, the conclusion must necessarily be accepted as true. For the syllogism to be valid, however, the subject of the major premise (all men) must be *distributed;* it can have no exceptions. As soon as you add a qualification of any sort, the syllogism is no longer valid.

> *Most men pay taxes.*
> *John is a man.*
> *Therefore John pays taxes.*

Here the conclusion doesn't follow. To show that John pays taxes we would also have to show that he is one of the "most men" who do.

Now let's look at a slightly trickier problem:

> *All dogs are animals.*
> *All cats are animals.*
> *Therefore all cats are dogs.*

It's obvious that the conclusion is not valid, but why? The form appears to be the same as that of our first example. If you look more closely, however, you will see that in the first example the *subject* of the major premise (men) is the *predicate* of the minor premise (man). This term is called the *middle term,* and its position is the key to a valid syllogism. The middle term must appear, in just this relationship, in both premises. It cannot appear in the conclusion. Moreover, in the conclusion the *minor term* must be the subject and the *major term* the predicate. Otherwise look what can happen:

> All dogs are animals.
> All cocker spaniels are dogs.
> Therefore all animals are cocker spaniels.

The categorical syllogism is the foundation of formal logic, but there are two other types of syllogisms that come up occasionally. The *hypothetical syllogism* has as its major premise a conditional proposition:

> If I am a man, then I am mortal.
> I am a man.
> Therefore I am mortal.

In the *disjunctive syllogism* the major premise contains two alternatives, at least one of which is true:

> I am either mortal or immortal.
> I am not immortal.
> Therefore I am mortal.

Each of these types has its own rules of validity.

In the examples above it is easy to tell whether the syllogism is valid or not. However, invalid syllogisms are not so easy to recognize when they are buried in rhetoric. Look at this example:

> Government investigations have fairly well established the fact that the Communist Party has supported the Negro revolution right from the very beginning. There is considerable evidence to show that the Communists have provided both leadership and financial backing. In the violent demonstrations on college campuses all over the country the students have consistently supported the cause of the black revolutionaries. It is plain that the students involved in these demonstrations are inspired by the Communist doctrine.

If you read this carefully you will see that it is actually a syllogism. But is it valid or invalid? Now, be careful. Don't make a judgment based on your own sentiments. Break the syllogism down into its essential parts:

> Communists support the Negro revolution.
> Student demonstrators support the Negro revolution.
> Therefore student demonstrators are Communists.

As you can see, the form here is the same as our example that said all cats are dogs.

This may seem to be a pretty slick way to analyzing arguments, but there are some pitfalls. For example, it is entirely possible for a syllogism to be valid even when the conclusion is untrue. Suppose you are a young man nineteen years old and your father tells you this:

> No, son, you can't have the car tonight. I've been doing a lot of reading on the subject of teen-age driving. The insurance reports clearly indicate that most automobile accidents are caused by male drivers between the ages of eighteen and twenty-five. There's no question about it. Young men in that age bracket are bad drivers, and since you are nineteen, that includes you.

Does he have a valid syllogism? As a matter of fact, he does.

> All young men between eighteen and twenty-five are bad drivers.
> You are a young man between eighteen and twenty-five.
> Therefore you are a bad driver.

Does this mean you have to give up and ride the bus? Not at all (provided your father is a reasonable man). You can't attack his logic but you can question the validity of his major premise. He has used a *distributed* term when it should have been *undistributed*. He can't say that *all* young men between eighteen and twenty-five are bad drivers (he can say it, but he can't back it up). All he can say is that *most* of them are bad drivers. Once you get him to change the "all" to "most," which qualifies his major premise, then you can attack his logic.

Understanding the difference between valid and invalid syllogisms can help you arrive at reasonable conclusions. If the concept is clearly sorted out in your own mind you can take it the next step and organize it into a pattern that can be understood by others.

ORGANIZING A SPEECH TO CONVINCE

A speech to convince is designed to make listeners accept a different point of view than that which they had previously believed. In doing this you will normally be either supporting or attacking the *status quo.*

STATUS QUO

In any speech that involves argumentation, it is important that you understand the prevailing conditions. Status quo is a term that means "the way things are." It could refer to the laws that are in effect, the generally accepted standards of morality, or any other present state or condition.

It is always necessary to examine the status quo carefully to be sure you are not just "tilting at windmills." If you are arguing for acceptance of something that has already been accepted or attacking an evil that does not exist, you not only have no case, but you are betraying your ignorance in the very area in which you are claiming to be informed.

Status quo is an important consideration when you are deciding whether to support or oppose a proposition that is on an election ballot. Sometimes propositions are not always clearly stated and if you are not careful you may wind up voting for something that you actually oppose. Remember this: Any time you vote "yes" on a proposition, you are voting in favor of a change in the status quo; when you vote "no" you are voting to retain the status quo. So it is necessary that you know what the status quo is. For example, the proposition may pertain to the construction of a new dam, and you may want to prevent it from being built. Status quo may be that permission to build the dam has been granted and the proposition would put a stop to it. So you would vote "yes" on the proposition because you are *opposed* to the dam.

Once you have this clear in your own mind you can begin to think of how you can make it clear to your audience. If the issue in question is confusing, you may want to start by describing the status quo.

THE NEED OR PROBLEM

Whether you are attacking or defending the status quo you will have to show the existence of some need or problem. If you like conditions the way they are and there is no threat to them, you do not have a controversial topic. In some instances the need or problem may be clear; in other cases you may have to explain to your audience the nature of the controversy. Let's say, for example, you wanted to give a speech on the rights of broadcasting stations to editorialize. Many people may not be aware that there are restrictions placed upon broadcasters that are not imposed upon newspapers. The Federal Communications Commission, which regulates the broadcasting industry, says that radio and television stations must abide by the conditions of the "Fairness Doctrine." If a station advocates one side of a controversial issue, "equal time" must be made available to those who wish to respond. Many broadcasters have contended that this restricts their ability to deal with controversial matters, and have called for the repeal of the Fairness Doctrine. In your speech you may wish to support or attack the Fairness Doctrine, but first you would have to tell what it is and explain how it has been challenged.

THE CAUSES

Once the problem has been identified, you can begin to look at the reasons behind it. Why is there such a thing as the Fairness Doctrine? The reason is that there are only a limited number of radio and television broadcasting frequencies available. If anyone who wanted to broadcast were able to do so, there would be no need for restrictions. But because of the technical limitations, the federal government has said that those who are granted broadcasting licenses must use their privilege fairly. The job of the speaker, then, is to analyze the *cause* of the limitation placed upon broadcasters to see if it is justifiable and to anticipate what would happen if that limitation were removed.

Sometimes causes are extremely complex and difficult to identify. Suppose, for example, you define a problem as the damage and loss that results from juvenile delinquency. You would be able to find many examples to illustrate the extent of the problem, but you might have some difficulty in describing the causes of juvenile delinquency. Keep in mind that causes are critical because they lead you into solutions. You could identify any number of causes—economic conditions, the high divorce rate, inadequate schools, legal restrictions, ineffective reform facilities, and so on. All of these suggest different answers to the problem. In order to have a convincing case, your solution must solve the problem by dealing with the causes you have described.

THE SOLUTION

In a speech to inform you may do nothing more than describe problems, but in a speech to convince you will be expected to offer solutions. What you will probably find when you begin putting together a speech to convince is that it is easier to identify problems than it is to solve them. Be realistic in what you are able to accomplish, and limit the scope of the problem you intend to solve. Along with the other benefits of a speech course that have previously been mentioned, you might develop an appreciation for those who have the responsibility to invent and implement solutions. Lawmakers, administrators, and people in positions of authority may not necessarily be incompetent or self-serving as we sometimes tend to believe—they may know something about the consequences of solutions that we have failed to consider.

Be as specific as you can in your recommendations. You may propose to your audience that we learn to love our fellow human beings, or that we fight to preserve our freedoms, but neither of these assertions has any functional application. It isn't hard to get people to accept some abstract virtue; the disagreement begins when you talk about the details. The trouble with avoiding details in the speech is that you may be asked about them in the question period. Your position should be clarified by that time so that your audience is not surprised by your answers. In your speech you may have said that unnecessary expenses must be cut, a statement with which your audience might thoroughly agree. But if you are forced to be specific about where those cuts should come, you might get considerable disagreement. Do not expect unanimous approval. Whenever you make specific declarations on a controversial issue you will gain the support of some and lose the support of others.

CONSTRUCTION OF A PRIMA FACIE CASE

So far we have spoken in general terms about the organization of a speech to convince. Now let us look at one specific kind of pattern called the *prima facie case*. Literally "prima facie" means "first face." It is the basic structure of a case that is evaluated separately from its evidence. In other words we say that a prima facie case is one that is constructed in such a way that it must be accepted unless one or more of its main contentions is rejected. In a court trial a prosecuting attorney is required to present a prima facie case against a defendant in order to obtain a conviction. The attorney must show that the person accused had the motive and the opportunity and was the only one who could have committed the crime. Then, if the evidence presented supports those contentions, the jury will have to find the defendant guilty. The defense will have to refute one or more of the main contentions to win an acquittal. The term "prima facie" does not refer to the quality of the evidence but to the inherent structure of the case itself. It is similar in some respects to the *syllogism*. If the major and minor premises of a valid syllogism are accepted as valid by the audience, they must necessarily accept the conclusion. The only way logically to deny the conclusion would be to deny the validity of either the major or the minor premise. Let us see how a prima facie case could be constructed which would advocate a new selective service act.

INTRODUCTION (attention-getting device)

If a major military conflict were to develop in Western Europe, United States fighting strength would be short by more than a million men.

THESIS STATEMENT

A national program of military selective service should be implemented before a crisis occurs.

BODY

   I The U.S. faces potentially dangerous military confrontations
      A Central America
      B The Persian Gulf
      C Berlin
  II Our present military forces are not prepared to deal with such confrontations
      A Insufficient number of active personnel
      B Inadequate number of reserves
      C Lack of personnel trained in needed skills
 III Incentives are not great enough to attract qualified men and women
      A Little sense of patriotism
      B Low pay compared to private sector
      C Most service personnel forced to "moonlight"
  IV Selective service would alleviate our weakness
      A Maintain our forces at necessary levels
      B Less expensive than increasing pay
      C Would be fairly administered
      D Build our reserves as well as active forces

CONCLUSION

Implementing selective service at this time would demonstrate to the world the strength of our resolve so that using military force would not be necessary.

These four contentions constitute a prima facie case. Each, of course, would have to be supported with concrete evidence. But an opponent to this case would have to succeed in refuting one or more of these contentions in order to logically deny the conclusion.

    Be careful not to make the mistake of thinking that a prima facie case is one that is irrefutable—there are always opposing arguments. By definition, all controversial issues have more than one side that can be reasonably and logically supported. If there were only one side, the issue would not be controversial. To illustrate this, Jimmy Carter, in his debate with Ronald Reagan, said that on the most critical matters, the experts usually are divided evenly. This is precisely why collegiate debate programs require students to defend alternately both sides of a given question. It is good practice to learn to debate either side of an argumentative topic. Understanding the rhetorical support of the opposition has many advantages: Your knowledge of the subject matter increases your credibility when you speak to an audience; you become more effective in your refutation when you have an understanding of the counterarguments; and the opinion that you eventually formulate will be one that is based upon sound consideration.

QUESTIONS FOR DISCUSSION

1 Do you believe that there is an absolute, or objective, truth? Do you act on absolute truth or on what you believe is true? In what sense can truth become what the most effective persuader makes it?

2 Where would you draw the line between coercion and persuasion? Which do you feel has been a greater influence on your behavior? At what point do threats and promises become instruments of coercion?

3 Which of the three modes of proof do you feel is the greatest factor in persuasion? Under what circumstances might emotional conviction override objective evidence in a decision?

4 What is the basis of charisma? Would you agree that Hitler was a charismatic speaker? If Martin Luther King had spoken the same words at some other point in history, would they have had the same impact?

5 The Roman teacher Quintilian described an orator as "a good man speaking well." How does the concept of a "good man" relate to a speaker's ethos? Is a sincere and ethical person necessarily a more effective speaker?

6 To what extent do you feel that speakers are responsible for the consequences of their influence? To what extent is a person responsible for the consequences of some casual comment? Do you feel that those who remain silent can disclaim all responsibility for consequences that their silence permitted?

SUGGESTED ACTIVITIES

1   List ten historical figures you admire. Explain what common characteristics they all had. Select one and tell how his or her life affected your own.

2   Have each member of the class tell an autobiographical anecdote. It can be either true or not. The rest of the class may ask questions and then try to determine whether or not the person is telling the truth. What generalizations can you make about someone who can lie convincingly? Is truth self-evident? If you perceived a lie, what were the factors that made it apparent?

6

PREPARING TO SPEAK

Your preparation as a public speaker began long before you picked up this book. It started the first time you decided to remember an experience so that you could tell someone else about it. All the information you gather as you look, listen, touch, taste, and smell contributes to the final product that will eventually become the speech you give to an audience. When Daniel Webster made his famous "Reply to Hayne" on the floor of Congress in 1830, he was asked how he could have made such an eloquent speech on the spur of the moment. His answer was, "I've been preparing that speech all my life."

PSYCHOLOGICAL PREPARATION

If you are like most people, you will have to prepare yourself psychologically to give a speech. Learning about the theory of oral communication can provide you with a greater understanding of what the study of speech is supposed to accomplish, but it may not help much in overcoming one of your biggest obstacles. The phenomenon we know as "speech fright" is known to everyone who has ever faced an audience. *The Book of Lists* ranks "fear of speaking to groups" as the greatest fear among most of the people surveyed.[1] While this information may not relieve your anxieties, you can be consoled by the fact that you have a lot of company. Speech fright need not be a debilitating factor in your communication. Anxiety causes adrenalin to flow and may sharpen both your wits and your perception. It also suggests that you regard the speaking situation as being one of importance. You may actually perform better than you would if you were completely relaxed and without tension. If, however, the speech anxiety rises to an intensity that interferes with your communication, you will want to take steps to relieve it. There is no "pink pill" or magic formula, but there are ways of *working* on the problem.

COGNITIVE RESTRUCTURING

Considerable success in dealing with speech fright has been achieved through the use of *cognitive restructuring*. This method is a "refined, systematic technique that alters the cognitive dimension of anxiety."[2] The student should work with a trained professional over a five- to eight-week period and should be willing to change both attitude and behavior. Cognitive restructuring is based on the notion "that maladaptive behavior is maintained by irrational self-statements. . . ."[3] It attempts to re-

[1] David Wallechinsky, Irving Wallace, and Amy Wallace, *The Book of Lists,* Bantam, New York, 1978, p. 469.

[2] William J. Fremouw and Michael D. Scott, "Cognitive Restructuring: An Alternative Method for the Treatment of Communication Apprehension," *Communication Education,* May 1979, p. 130.

[3] Ibid., p. 131.

place the negative messages people often give to themselves with more positive ones that contribute to effective communication behavior. All too frequently students come into class on the day of their speech reciting to themselves such admonitions as, "I'll never be able to do this . . . " and, "I'm going to forget everything I planned to say. . . ." What happens is that they invariably bring about just what they predict.

Cognitive restructuring is accomplished through a four-step process.[4] First, students are provided with a thorough rationale and purpose for the training. It is important to accept the fact that apprehension is a *learned reaction* and therefore is subject to modification. Each student is asked to describe the particular communication situations that create anxiety. "These descriptions not only serve to involve the subjects, but also can be used as relevant examples in later training seminars."[5] The second step is for students to identify specific negative self-statements which contribute to the anxiety. These statements are then examined to see if there is any validity to their content. The third step is for students to learn to replace the negative statements with positive ones. These may be statements that facilitate behavioral changes such as, "I can speak well when I speak slowly." But in all cases, the emphasis is upon students giving themselves encouragement that leads to confidence. The final step is practice. Students role-play the situations that they have identified as those which cause anxiety. A program such as this, when pursued conscientiously and directed by a well-trained therapist, can be extremely effective in reducing anxiety.

If you do not have access to professional guidance, you may have to take matters into your own hands and set up your own program for reducing apprehension.

PREPARE THE SPEECH THOROUGHLY

There is no substitute for this step toward anxiety reduction. Much of the time fear comes about as a result of uncertainty over adequacy of preparation. Make sure you have clear, concise assertions supported by interesting, specific examples. Have your organizational pattern well in mind, and go over your ideas

[4] Ibid., p. 132.

[5] Ibid.

several times before you deliver the speech. Don't practice on your audience; practice on someone else beforehand. Be sure that you have well-organized notes, that you are dressed comfortably and suitably for the occasion, and that you arrive on time. In other words, avoid the *obvious* pitfalls that may cause you discomfort or anxiety.

VISUALIZE WHAT YOU WANT TO DO

Well before the speech, begin picturing in your mind the way you want it to be. Be as specific as you can in creating an image of yourself delivering the speech, and always think of the positive characteristics. Imagine yourself being confident, articulate, and poised. Keep that image in your mind every time you think about giving the speech, until it is thoroughly etched as the person you know yourself to be. The value of this exercise is that it promotes behavior that will lead to fulfillment of the image. We all like to behave in a way that is consistent with what we perceive ourselves to be. The creative imagination is capable of conjuring up any picture at all without cost and with very little effort. The pictures are completely within your control—they can be anything you want them to be. If you view yourself as being self-conscious and disorganized, that is precisely how you will appear. Henry Ford said, "Whether a man believes he will succeed or fail, he is right."

PRACTICE PROGRESSIVE RELAXATION

The night before the speech take time for a relaxation exercise. Sit in a comfortable chair away from any distractions and bright lights. Start by taking several deep breaths and exhaling slowly. With each breath, deepen the relaxation. To go through the progressive relaxation process, start by focusing your attention on the muscles in your feet. Flex the muscles and then let them relax. Do the same thing with your legs, and then gradually move up through your body, flexing the muscles and relaxing them. When you are thoroughly relaxed, take a few minutes to enjoy the experience; then begin thinking about the speech.

Again, visualize all of the positive aspects you can think of in regard to giving the speech. While you are in a relaxed state, get a clear picture of yourself standing in front of the audience, speaking in a strong voice and saying what you want to say. Visualize the audience listening to you and responding in a favorable fashion. Associate the positive image with your feeling of relaxation so that when you give the speech you will feel the same way.

EXERCISE YOUR VOICE

Whenever you can, practice speaking at the volume you will need when you deliver the speech. It may be uncomfortable to you at first to hear yourself talking that loud, but do it enough so that you will get used to it. On the morning of the speech stretch the vocal cords by talking, shouting, or singing out loud. You can do it in the shower if you want, but make sure your throat is not obstructed and that your voice can produce well-modulated tones.

All of these suggestions will help, but none of them will replace experience. Public speaking is an art that develops with practice—you have to do a lot of it before it becomes really comfortable.

METHODS OF DELIVERY

Every speaking situation is different, and to become proficient in public speaking you will have to develop versatility. There will be times when you will need to read from a printed page and other times when you will have to speak "off the cuff." The formality of the occasion is one of the main determinants in selecting a method of delivery. If your audience is small and informal you will probably choose to extemporize rather than read from a manuscript. Let's consider some of the methods of delivery.

READING FROM A MANUSCRIPT

Political speakers prefer to give their speeches this way for several reasons. There is less danger of their saying something they hadn't meant to say; the presentation is smooth and formal; and advance copy is available for the press. The disadvantages are that rapport with the audience is poor, and sometimes the audience suspects that the speaker is reading someone else's words.

MEMORIZING

This is an excellent method for someone who plans to give the same speech a number of times. Usually the speech will improve each time it is given. The speaker can use exactly the planned words with no loss in audience contact. Often, however, the speech sounds memorized, especially the first few times it is given, and again, the audience may wonder whether the words are someone else's. The main difficulty is that the speaker is generally concentrating on the words rather than the ideas, and is lost if the next word is forgotten. Moreover, it is difficult to memorize a speech, especially a long one. The time could be better spent in other forms of speech preparation.

SPEAKING IMPROMPTU

An impromptu speech is one that is given with no advance preparation. It takes considerable skill and experience to be able to speak effectively on the spur of the moment. Impromptu speaking can be fun, and it is excellent practice. However, if the speaker has no ideas or information on the topic, an impromptu speech can be a great waste of everybody's time.

In case your instructor assigns an impromptu speech as an exercise, you should know something about it. Very little has been written on how to give an impromptu speech. Most writers merely advise you not to let yourself get caught in a situation where you have to give one. In one sense this isn't bad advice. If you can anticipate being called on to speak, even by a few minutes, you can begin organizing your thoughts. If you are a reasonably well-organized person, if you know what you believe and why you believe it, if you have expressed your beliefs in conversation with your friends, the chances are that you will have little difficulty in expressing the same ideas to a group of people.

The only kind of impromptu speech that makes any sense is one on a topic you know something about. There is no point in making your audience sit there and listen to meaningless noises just because you feel compelled to use up the time. There are occasions when a courteous decline is preferable to a gallant attempt.

The best way to prepare for impromptu speaking is to keep yourself well-informed on important current topics and get used to discussing them with your friends. Conversation is a good way of testing your ideas and practicing clear, well-organized verbal expression.

Pay attention.   Whenever you attend a meeting or gathering of any kind, stay alert and pay attention to what is being said. Think in terms of how you would respond if you were asked to comment on something the speaker had just said.

Give a direct response.   Often the impromptu speech will be a response to some question. Begin by answering the question as directly as you can; then qualify and develop your answer. Don't leave your audience wondering what your position is, so that they have to ask the question the second time.

Keep it short.   No one expects a full-length speech on the spur of the moment. If the chairman had wanted you to give a major address, you would have been included on the program. Keep your remarks short and to the point. Don't go off on a tangent. Keep the central idea in mind the whole time you are talking, and don't deviate from it.

Keep the end in sight.   The hardest thing about an impromptu speech is ending it. Remember that all speeches must have conclusions, whether they are prepared or not. To be sure your impromptu speech doesn't just wither away and trail off into silence, plan your concluding statement as soon as you start talking. It should be something similar to your opening statement. Anticipate your last sentence before you come to it, so you will be able to finish up in a strong, dynamic tone.

Impromptu speaking is not easy. The people who do it well are the ones who do it often and have a large fund of ideas and information to draw on. In this respect good impromptu speeches are not impromptu at all. They reflect ideas that have been given considerable thought and have probably been expressed before in an unstructured situation of informal discourse.

SPEAKING EXTEMPORANEOUSLY

The extemporaneous speech is prepared in advance but is then delivered spontaneously. Extemporaneous speakers may use brief notes to jog the memory, but the notes cover only the ideas and information, not the words which will express them. They have carefully planned and organized what they have to say, but choose words as they go along. Hence they can express themselves spontaneously, with occasional reference to notes to help them move smoothly from one idea to the next.

Extemporaneous speaking is the method on which a speech course usually focuses, because it combines the best features of all the other methods of delivery. It allows the speaker to organize thoughts and information for the most effective presentation and provides the same kind of audience contact an impromptu speech provides.

PREPARING MATERIALS

Public speaking is an art that requires not just the voice, but often the use of physical materials as well. In addition to talking about the rhetorical aspect of the speech, we need to discuss the logistics.

USING NOTE CARDS

It's a good idea to prepare note cards in addition to your outline. Your instructor will probably want to have the outline while you are giving your speech. From your own standpoint, however, cards are a lot easier to handle while you are speaking. They can be held inconspicuously in one hand; you don't have to put them down if you want to move around or gesture to your audience. You can hold them up to look at without blocking your view of the audience or having to look down and away from them. And cards won't rattle the way a sheet of paper does if your hand just happens to shake a bit.

Your cards can be 3 × 5, or 4 × 6, or 5 × 8—whatever size is most comfortable for you. Here are a few rules regarding their preparation:

Type or write legibly.   The print should be dark enough so that you will be able to see it clearly at a glance.

Underline important ideas.   Also, put quotation marks around direct quotations, and always include some note on the source of a quotation.

Write on only one side of the card. Don't use both sides. If you have to turn a card over, you may forget whether or not you have already covered the material on the other side. Remember that you are likely to be under some pressure when you are giving your speech.

Don't write a complete transcript of your speech on the note cards. If you do, you will be strongly tempted to read it, and your audience contact will suffer. You won't get the experience you need in extemporizing, and you will probably also get a low grade on your speech. Put on the cards only key words and phrases to serve as reminders of your ideas.

USING AUDIO AND VISUAL MATERIALS

The beginning speaker will find some advantage in using audio and visual materials in a speech. Working with physical objects gives you a chance to do something with your hands to release some of the nervous energy that often is a result of stage fright. In addition the materials provide "cues" so that you are less likely to forget what you want to say. Let's look first at the use of two-dimensional aids—charts, pictures, maps, and so on. When they are used effectively they can be a big help in explaining your point. If they aren't used properly, however, they can just get in your way. There are some specific points to bear in mind in preparing your displays:

Be sure they are large enough to be seen. Calculate the size and position of your audience and prepare your chart or map so that the person in the farthest corner of the room can see it. This is just as important as speaking loudly enough to be heard.

Keep them simple. A display that is too "busy" will distract your audience. If they can't immediately grasp everything that is on it, they may spend their time trying to decipher it instead of listening to you. Explain everything that needs to be explained and clearly point out how the information you are showing supports what you are saying. Try to avoid including anything on your display that isn't covered in your speech.

Be sure they are neat. The visual aids that you use become a part of your speech. They say something about your attitude toward the audience. Carelessly prepared material indicates that you didn't consider the matter important enough to go to any great bother. In that case, your audience may take the same attitude.

Whatever visual aids you use, be sure you know exactly how you are going to use them. Otherwise you may find yourself tripping over your own material. Figure out where you are going to put your display, how you are going to get it there, and where you are going to stand when you refer to it. Plan when you are going to display your material and how long you are going to leave it up. Here are some tips:

Place your display high enough and in a position where it can be seen.   Generally classrooms have hooks and clips to hang things on, but you may have to bring an easel. Position the display so that you can stand to one side of it, without blocking the view of anyone in the audience. This may take some thought.

If possible, don't display your material until you are ready to discuss it.   It may be distracting if you put it up too soon. When you rehearse your speech, practice setting your material up while you are talking. It will take some practice to be able to do this quickly and smoothly, but you don't want to leave your audience in silence any longer than you have to.

Plan how and when you are going to take your material down.   If you feel that your display may distract the audience after you have moved on to your next point, take it down at some convenient time. Sometimes, however, it is a good idea to leave it up in case your audience wants to refer back to it later.

SPEECHES WITH THREE-DIMENSIONAL AIDS

The possibilities here are limited only by your imagination. There may be some restrictions, however, on what you can bring into the classroom. For example, firearms are generally prohibited unless the bolt or firing pin has been removed. Don't bring in any article that is illegal, no matter what you plan to say about it. Animals may or may not be acceptable, depending on the inclination of your instructor, but a word of caution—they are quite unpredictable and may wind up stealing the show.

The same considerations apply as for two-dimensional aids, with a few further ones:

Make sure the demonstration works.   When you practice your speech, include the demonstration in your rehearsal. If you are going to show the audience how safety bindings work on skis, be sure yours work the way they are supposed to. It's embarrassing to start out with a big buildup and then have your demonstration misfire.

Pass objects around only when necessary.   Sometimes it is advantageous to pass around something that is too small for everyone to see from their seats. Be sure to explain what it is first. However, don't pass around any more things than you have to, and don't have too many objects in circulation at the same time. Whoever is looking at the object is probably not paying attention to you at the moment. If you have a lot of things in circulation, you may lose a good portion of your audience.

SPEECHES WITH BODILY PERFORMANCE

Sometimes your own activity may be the demonstration. Some unusual speeches of this sort have been given. One student crushed grapes with her bare feet while she discussed wine making. Another gave his speech by radio while he was flying 2,000 feet above the campus. Another prepared hors d'oeuvres for the entire class in eight minutes. The important thing, of course, is not the uniqueness of your approach, but how good your speech is.

For some speeches you may want to use members of the audience. One student supplied squirt guns filled with different-colored paints to several members of the audience and had them take random shots at a piece of canvas to illustrate a possible new art form. If you plan to use participants from the audience, it's a good idea to line them up in advance. If you spring something on your audience with no warning, you may not get any volunteers, and if you have to pick "volunteers," they may be too embarrassed to participate with any enthusiasm. There are also speeches in which the entire audience may be asked to take part. Some speakers have had the audience join them in yoga exercises, or analyze the lines in the palms of their hands. This type of speech has the advantage of getting everyone actively involved in the communication process, but you have to be careful that your audience doesn't get too carried away.

Remember that the success of your demonstration will depend to a large extent on the quality of your end product. If you are showing how pottery is made on a potter's wheel, you should have something fairly impressive to show your audience when you finish. The impact of your speech is weakened if you have to apologize for an object you produced. Incidentally, you will find it very difficult to perform a complicated operation and talk to an audience at the same time, and if the performance takes a great deal of energy, you may find yourself panting for breath while you are trying to speak. You had better check to be sure you can carry it off. If you can't, pick another topic.

Whatever type of demonstration you use, don't forget that you are in a speech class. Your demonstration is an aid to your speech, not a substitute for it. No matter how skilled you may be in the area you are demonstrating, what you will be judged on is your skill in speech making.

SPEECHES WITH AUDIOVISUAL AIDS

You may sometimes have access to audiovisual equipment. Not all speeches are improved by the use of audiovisual aids. If you do decide to use them be sure you are thoroughly checked out on the equipment before you give your speech.

The slide projector.   This can be a good aid if you have good pictures. Don't show too many—and have something to say about each one. The disadvantage is that you will not be able to maintain good contact with your audience in a dark room.

The overhead projector.   This is one of the most effective of the audiovisual aids. The room doesn't have to be dark for clear projection, and you can face your audience while you use it. However, you will have to obtain or make your own transparencies.

The opaque projector.   With this machine you can show pictures in books and magazines, and even flat objects such as coins. It has two big disadvantages—often the machine is noisy in operation, and the room must be quite dark for effective projection.

The phonograph.   If you want to use selections from phonograph records, go ahead and do so. But remember that you will have trouble finding just the right spot to put the needle down, especially if your hand is shaking a bit.

The tape recorder.   If you are planning to use music, speech, or sound effects, a tape recorder is easier to use than a phonograph. It can be stopped and started more smoothly, and the right spot on the tape can be found with greater ease.

The motion-picture projector.   Film can be worked into a speech just as slides can. The disadvantage is the same as with the slide projector—the room must be dark, and contact with the audience is at a minimum.

Remember that verbal communication is only one of the ways in which people receive messages. Your objective as a speaker is to communicate a message to your audience, and the more ways of communicating you can incorporate in your speech, the more effective your communication will be. If you can augment your spoken message by effective appeals to the visual and other senses, it is certainly to your advantage to do so.

RADIO AND TELEVISION

The ancient art of rhetoric has been significantly modified in the past eighty years by the development of electronic media. Before this century a speaker could not effectively address more than a few hundred people at a time, and then only by means of a powerful voice. But with electronic aid the speaker can be heard and seen by thousands and even millions of people while talking in a conversational tone of voice. Franklin D. Roosevelt was one of the first politicians to use radio effectively when he began his famous "fireside chats." He spoke quietly and calmly, in contrast to the flamboyance that characterized most public speakers of the time. Others followed suit and the style of all political speechmaking began to change.

THE USE OF MICROPHONES

A microphone can be an intimidating thing until you become accustomed to using it. A sensitive microphone picks up all the sounds you make—even the ones you may want not to be heard. It is a valuable tool for the speaker, but like all tools, it needs to be used properly.

1. Speak into the microphone at a slight angle. Try to stay within 5 or 6 inches, and keep the distance as constant as possible.

2. Don't mutter or whisper to yourself or make other, nonverbal, sounds that you don't want the audience to hear.

3. Don't handle the microphone; it will rattle. If it needs to be adjusted, let someone else do it for you. If you have to adjust it yourself, don't try to talk while you are doing so. Test it after it has been adjusted by speaking, not blowing into it.

TELEVISION CAMERAS

The use of television has become so prevalent in our society that it is difficult to avoid. The medium is no longer the exclusive preserve of the big networks. Local stations are able to take portable cameras into almost any situation to provide news coverage. Schools and colleges commonly use television for instructional purposes; industry, too, uses it as a training tool; and home units are becoming more and more popular. Again, some techniques are important for effective use of the television medium.

1 Look at the person to whom you are talking. If that person is the viewer, look at the camera. If there are other people on camera with you, talk to them. Never talk to the monitor screen regardless of how tempting it may be to look at yourself.

2 Avoid sudden or unpredictable movements. If you stand up quickly or walk off to one side, you will move right out of the picture. If you move suddenly toward or away from the camera, you will go out of focus.

3 Pay attention to your posture whether standing or sitting. Slouching, scratching your head, tapping your foot—ungainly attitudes and unnecessary movements distract the viewer. Remember the television screen is able to bring you up close to the audience.

All of the electronic media should be viewed by the speaker not as a threat, but as an enhancement of the communication art, providing an opportunity to deliver the message more clearly to more people.

QUESTIONS FOR DISCUSSION

1   How effective do you think cognitive restructuring can be? Is it possible for speech fright to be overcome? Are better speeches given by people who do not experience speech fright?

2   Do you feel that a speech which is read or memorized sounds insincere? On what factors do you base your judgment of the sincerity of a speaker?

3   How effective are audiovisual materials? Are there times when you would choose not to use visual aids? In what way do visual aids interfere with audience contact?

4   What effect have the mass media had upon speech making? Is a speech on television as effective as one delivered to a "live" audience?

SUGGESTED ACTIVITIES

1   If your school has videotape recording equipment, stand in front of the camera and pretend to deliver a speech from a sheet of paper; then do the same thing with note cards. Watch the playback and see which visual impression you like better.

2   Write several speech topics on the chalkboard. Have each member of the class select one, and do a three-minute impromptu speech.

3   Bring a small object to class. Give it to the person next to you and have him or her use it in an impromptu speech.

7

DELIVERING THE MESSAGE

You may spend many hours researching material and preparing your outline, and then produce only a mediocre speech because you have failed to take the easiest step of all—practicing your delivery. Perhaps you feel that rehearsing a speech will change your presentation from honest communicating into a "performance" or an "acting" job. True, a good speech should be natural, an honest reflection of your personality. However, remember that public speaking is structured, and the goal of structured communication is to convey the greatest amount of information on the stated topic as quickly as possible. You don't do your audience any favor by taking up their time with irrelevant personal matters, and they probably won't listen to you if you do. For that matter, practice in structured speaking will help you improve your informal discourse as well. The more clearly and succinctly you can say what you have to say, without a lot of superfluous side-tracking, the more people in any situation are going to listen with interest.

FACING YOUR AUDIENCE

You probably have spoken to groups before, but you may not have taken the time to analyze what you were doing. Out of all the suggestions that will be made in this chapter, you will select the ones that work best for you and develop a style that is uniquely your own. The important thing is to be *intentional*—to communicate precisely the message that you want your audience to hear.

LEARNING TO STAND

There will certainly be occasions when you can speak to a group while you are seated, or even perched on the edge of a desk. First, however, you had better learn how to stand—on both feet. Standing with your weight on one foot is no great crime. The problem is that you then tend to shift to the other one, and you are likely to end up rocking back and forth without being aware of it. Your audience will be aware of it. With a firm foundation you are less likely to distract either yourself or your audience with awkward poses.

Avoid the temptation to lean on things. Tables, chairs, and lecterns are not crutches. To speak effectively you should display a certain amount of physical vitality, and leaning on the furniture gives the impression that you just can't summon up the necessary energy.

LEARNING TO MOVE

Once you get set behind the lectern or the desk, don't feel that you have taken root there. Feel free to move around as long as the movement has some purpose. Don't pace the floor just to dissipate energy, but do move when there is a reason to do so. You may want to walk to the chalkboard to write something down, or turn once in a while to face a part of the audience that can't see you too well.

One particular reason for moving is to close the distance between you and your audience in order to emphasize an important point. The effectiveness of communication varies with the distance between the speaker and the audience. As the distance is decreased, a greater impression of intimacy is created. You may have noticed this effect when a speaker steps out from behind the lectern and moves toward the audience.

Just as you needn't feel glued to one spot, don't feel that your elbows are glued to your ribs. If you can, rehearse your speech in front of a mirror. Experiment with different kinds of gestures to see how they look, but don't plan them for specific points in the speech. Gestures, in order to be effective, must be naturally motivated. The important thing is to overcome the reluctance you may have to use gestures at all. Use your speech class as a laboratory to investigate the effects of various positions and movements. See for yourself what kinds of results you get.

MAINTAINING EYE CONTACT

Ever since Julius Fast wrote his book called *Body Language* there has been a popular awareness of nonverbal communication. What do we say with our bodies and facial expressions? One study conducted by Ralph V. Exline confirmed an assumption we have made for a long time about eye contact: Most people perceive that "If while you are speaking, you look at the listener, you may be signaling, 'I am certain of what I am saying.' "[1] Other studies have shown that eye contact with the audience is one of the factors people use in determining the sincerity of a speaker.

Eye contact should be a *result* of sincerity, not a *cause* in creating it. (Remember what we said about cause and effect relationships.) Looking at an audience does not *cause* you to be sincere; it is something you do because you *are* sincere. Unfortunately, however, the sincerity you feel may not be communicated unless you maintain eye contact.

Look at faces as much as you can when you speak to an audience. Don't look over the tops of their heads or stare off into space. Above all, don't fix your eyes on your notes or on the lectern. Remember, you are talking to people, not to a piece of

[1] Julius Fast, *Body Language*, M. Evans and Company, Inc., New York, 1970, p. 151.

furniture. While you are speaking, look for the friendly faces—the ones that are expressing interest and acceptance. Talking to them will build your confidence.

USING YOUR VOICE

Now that you have some idea of the factors involved in facing your audience, what happens when you open your mouth to speak? Here too, there are some points you will have to take into consideration in a structured, public-speaking situation.

VOLUME

One of the things you are going to have to get used to is that public speaking requires more volume than ordinary conversation. At first you may feel that you are shouting, but you will soon become accustomed to the sound of your voice at that level. You can run a simple test by yourself if you have a tape recorder with a volume meter on it. With a microphone connected, put the tape machine in record mode and turn the volume all the way up. Now back off about fifteen feet from the microphone and talk. You should get some reading on the meter; if you don't, talk louder. That's about the volume you'll need to reach a roomful of 25 or 30 people.

If you discover that you have the volume but don't want to use it, the reason may be that you are uncertain of your material. You may be saying to yourself, "I don't want to talk too loud, because somebody hearing me might hold me responsible for what I am saying." If that's the case, put more effort into preparing your message. An increase in confidence is often sufficient to increase volume.

PITCH

Pitch problems can be difficult to overcome, but the first step is to identify them. There are two basic kinds—the *monotone* and the *patterned pitch.* The monotone speaker, sometimes labeled "Johnny one-note," is wearing to listen to, like the same key sounded over and over on a piano. As a result, it becomes difficult to concentrate on what is being said even when the speaker's material is good. If you have this kind of pitch problem, try rehearsing your speech with a tape recorder, and practice varying your pitch. This is often easier to do if you increase your volume, your rate of delivery, and your general level of enthusiasm.

A speaker with patterned pitch has what is known as a "sing-song voice." It goes up or down at regular intervals, and the audience tends to concentrate on the pattern rather than on the words it is hearing. Often this problem is a result of having memorized the speech. Again, a tape recorder is helpful for identifying the pattern and practicing to overcome it.

VOCAL EMPHASIS

Vocal emphasis is important for the sake of oratory, but it is often essential to clarify your meaning. Look at this sentence:

I didn't say he stole my book.

It contains seven words in the English language, and since we know the meaning of all the words, we might say we know the meaning of the sentence, right? Well, take another look at it. It has seven different meanings, depending on which word you emphasize. Try it. Repeat the sentence to yourself, emphasizing each of the words in order. This is just one more of the many ways you might be misunderstood, when you thought what you were saying was perfectly clear.

When you just said this sentence to yourself, you probably said the emphasized word a little louder and at a slightly higher pitch than the other words in the sentence. You may also have paused slightly just before the emphasized word. In general, vocal emphasis entails some kind of vocal change to set off what you are emphasizing from the surrounding material.

RATE OF DELIVERY

People can listen faster than you can talk, and if they are left for long without something to listen to, their attention will wander. You will probably have to speak faster than you usually do in casual conversation. There is no one rate of delivery that is best for all speakers, but you should talk as fast as you can without stumbling over words or slurring syllables. For some of you this will be about 90 words a minute, and for others it may be as high as 200 words a minute. Remember, however, that the rate itself is not as important as your clarity; every word and every syllable must be understood.

SPEAKING TO YOUR AUDIENCE

When you deliver your speech you will have to consider how you are going to move from one idea to the next. Your speech should have continuity and should flow smoothly from beginning to end. However, the need for transitions is not just an artistic one. Although you know in your own mind how what you are saying relates logically to your last point, the relationship may not be so clear to your audience. They are more likely to grasp what you are saying if they can see how your information fits into place, instead of having to stop and figure it out for themselves.

There are two kinds of transitions you can employ—*rhetorical transitions* and *vocal transitions*.

THE RHETORICAL TRANSITION

This is a sentence or phrase that links what was said before with that which is to come. There are a number of perfectly acceptable stock transitions:

> *And so we can see that . . .*
> *Now let's take a look at. . .*
> *By the same token, . . .*
> *In the final analysis, . . .*

Such transitional phrases clearly indicate the organization of main ideas and their relationship to each other. They point out at each stage the direction the speaker is now going to take. The stock phrases will do if your only concern is flawless organization, but your speech will be more interesting if you vary the formula a bit. You don't have to include rhetorical transitions in your outline, but if you do, put them in parentheses.

THE VOCAL TRANSITION

One advantage the speaker has over the writer is that the speaker can use vocal transitions to indicate a "shift in gears." There isn't any rigid formula for making vocal transitions; this is a technique that will have to be developed with experimentation and practice. Generally, however, the vocal transition is effected chiefly through a change in volume and pitch. Usually a speaker will drop his or her voice at the end of one idea, pause slightly, and then begin the next statement at a higher volume and pitch. Often the vocal transition is used in conjunction with the rhetorical transition.

For your vocal transitions to be effective, you will have to think ahead of what you are saying. When you come to the last sentence in a discussion, and especially the last sentence in your speech, you must anticipate it far enough in advance to give yourself a chance to drop down to the period. If you get caught short, you are likely to leave the audience hanging in midair by ending your speech on an upward inflection. This, of course, is what makes extemporizing difficult. You must keep track not only of what you are saying, but of what you have just said as well as what you are going to say next.

LANGUAGE

Nothing will mark you more quickly as immature than the use of immature language—words such as "swell," "guy," "stuff." The use of contemporary vernacular can sometimes be an effective means of establishing rapport with our audience, but like anything else in your speech, it should be used selectively. You may not want your audience to consider you stuffy, but neither do you want them to think you are incapable of expressing yourself in standard English.

THE IMAGE YOU PROJECT

Now that you have some ideas about how to put your speech across, let's give some thought to the factors involved in putting yourself across. The message your audience receives and their willingness to accept it is going to be determined in large measure by their perception of you as a person—by your ethos. To be an effective speaker you must not only possess the qualities that will win their respect, you must also project them. The characteristics of ethos are elusive, but there are some fundamental points on which the audience will base their judgment.

SINCERITY

This is the primary basis on which an audience will judge your integrity as a speaker. It would be convenient if sincerity were self-evident, if we could always tell the "good guys" from the "bad guys." Unfortunately sincerity and someone else's belief in that sincerity are two different things. You have probably heard people say that they can always tell when a speaker really believes in what he or she is saying, or that an astute audience can detect insincerity. The evidence, however, reveals the contrary. People may *say* they can perceive sincerity, but their guesses are wrong half of the time. What they are observing are characteristics they attribute to sincerity—maintaining a relaxed posture, using conventional gestures, reflecting a pleasant mood, and looking at the audience most of the time. These are all techniques effective speakers can learn, whether they are sincere or not.

It should be clear by now that just being sincere isn't going to be enough. You can't assume that your feeling of sincerity will magically transmit itself to the audience with no effort on your part, and that the techniques of projecting sincerity are needed only by the insincere. Regardless of your own convictions, you may find that you are projecting quite a different image to your audience. This kind of situation frequently arises when you are concentrating on the words of your speech rather than the ideas. You may use expressions that stand out from your usual way of speaking. This discrepancy is likely to register with the audience as phoniness. One way to avoid this situation is to practice extemporizing rather than memorizing.

AFFABILITY

Another major factor in the audience's evaluation of what you say is how well they like you. Think back over your own experience. Haven't you ever rejected what someone said just because you didn't like him, or taken someone's advice because she was your best friend?

In one study with young children, five popular and five unpopular children were picked to perform simple tasks in front of the class. The five popular ones were taken aside and told privately that when their instructions were announced they were to do exactly the opposite of whatever they were instructed to do. The tasks were then announced and performed according to plan, and the children who were watching were told to write down the names of the children who had performed correctly. You guessed it. They named the five children they liked. In case you think this phenomenon is restricted to children, in another study a group of teachers were asked to list the children they liked and those they disliked; then a number of spelling tests that they had already graded were examined. It was found that the teachers had overlooked a significant number of spelling errors on the pages of those they liked.

You may not be happy with the idea that people will accept or reject what you say on the basis of whether they like you or not, but often it happens that way. The rapport you establish with your audience in the first few minutes of your speech may well determine its success.

THE MESSAGE FROM THE AUDIENCE

In your first attempts at public speaking you probably will have all you can do to concentrate on what you are saying to your audience without having to worry about what they are saying to you. As you gain experience and become more confident in yourself, you can start giving some thought to the message from your audience. In some cases you may be able to make spontaneous adjustments to them as you observe their reaction. Be careful, however, about going off on a tangent that you had not planned. You can easily get bogged down in unnecessary detail that is not relevant to your topic. Just as impromptu speaking is based on a backlog of experience, effective "spontaneous" adjustments require a certain amount of forethought.

Before we discuss the more subtle aspects of adjusting to an audience, let's examine the area in which their response will be the most apparent.

THE QUESTION PERIOD

Most of your speeches will probably be followed by a question period. This can be the most challenging aspect of a speech, and perhaps the most fruitful in terms of communication. It is also the best way for you to find out how your audience reacted to what you had to say. Just as there are guidelines for making your prepared message effective, so there are guidelines for handling a question period:

Be sure there is no break in your relationship with the audience.   The question period is just as much a part of your speech as the prepared portion. Don't deliver your speech with polished formality and then take the attitude during the question period that now you can relax and really talk to your audience. This is what you were supposed to have been doing all along.

Be sure you are armed with plenty of information on your subject.   It is at this time that your audience will not only have a chance to clarify any points of confusion, but will also be able to find out if you really know what you are talking about. You should be able to add new information and use different examples in your replies, so that you aren't just rehashing what you have already said.

Anticipate as many of the questions as you can.   If you are well prepared there should be few questions that take you by surprise. It is especially important in a speech to convince that you be prepared for questions and objections based on the opposing view. Don't let the audience think you have been caught off guard by a challenging question. Let them know that you welcome the opportunity to clarify your point.

Direct your answers to the whole audience.   Don't address your response only to the person who asked the question. Remember that the question period is part of your speech, and you are speaking to the whole audience. First of all, make sure everyone has heard the question; if you have any doubt about this, repeat the question so they *can* hear it (and have the questioner confirm your paraphrase). Then answer so that everyone can hear. This problem arises most frequently when the questioner is sitting in the front row—and the people in the front row are the ones most likely to ask questions.

Be succinct.   This applies just as much to your response to a question as to the prepared portion of your speech. A long-winded dissertation in reply to one question is uncalled for and inappropriate. It has the effect of discouraging others from asking questions.

Get lots of people involved.   The question period should be dynamic; it should move rapidly and involve as many people as there is time for. There are always people in the audience who will want to make speeches of their own, or will ask you one question after another. Don't let them. You may even have to interrupt once you get the gist of a question. Answer it and then move on to someone else. If you get caught in a dialog with one person, you will lose the rest.

Stay on top of the situation.   The question period is part of the public-speaking situation, not a group discussion. You should get lots of people involved, but be sure they don't take over the proceedings and start addressing questions to each other rather than to you. This can easily happen if you allow long questions or fail to reply to each question. If you notice private exchanges beginning to develop between members of the audience, this is the time to make a strong point as emphatically as you can to regain their attention. If it doesn't work, you might as well sit down.

Know when to stop.   Since the question period is an important part of your speech, be sure you allow enough time for it. The length of a question period depends entirely on the circumstances. Often there are time limitations; other speakers may be scheduled or your audience may be on their lunch hour. If your time is not restricted, you will have to judge how long to allow questions to continue. As long as the whole audience seems interested, keep going, but don't let one or two questioners drag things on until the rest get bored. Try to get in the last word yourself; it's not a bad idea to save some closing remark as an exit line.

INDICATORS OF AUDIENCE RESPONSE

An audience will always give you some kind of feedback during your speech, either directly or indirectly. However, it is not always easy to interpret.

OVERT RESPONSE

There are certain traditional ways in which an audience demonstrates its response to a speaker. The most direct response is that strange custom of beating the hands together to show approval and appreciation. Applause in fact serves a very useful purpose. First of all, it unites an audience in a common activity and allows a large group of people to participate simultaneously in the communication process; they are all saying something together. Second, it gives speakers concrete evidence of where they stand. One of the frightening things about facing an audience is that you don't really know how they are going to take you. A round of applause reassures you that you are among friends. Laughter when you tell a joke has the same effect; it lets you know that the audience is with you. This kind of overt response does a lot to put both the speaker and the audience at ease.

COVERT RESPONSE

While some kinds of audience response are unmistakable in meaning, there are also covert responses. Some are easier to spot than others, but not necessarily any easier to interpret. Yawning, whispered conversations, nodding, or shaking of the head may indicate individual reactions, but they don't tell much about the audience as a whole. And as individual reactions, they may be deceiving. A person who is yawning or whose eyes are closed may be listening more intently than someone who looks wide awake. The woman in the second row who keeps nodding her head may not actually be expressing agreement; she may just be trying to follow what you are saying.

What message would you get when people in the audience are squirming around in their seats? You must have been told as a child to "sit still and pay attention." Is there actually any correlation between sitting still and paying attention? There is at least some evidence that there may be a connection. In one study the seats in an auditorium were outfitted with a "wiggle meter," which recorded any movements of the occupants. A number of audiences were subjected to different kinds of speeches, some dull and some interesting. The wiggle meter registered more movement during the dull speeches than during the interesting ones.[2]

You have probably also heard people say that they could tell what other people were thinking by the expression on their faces. This may not be a reliable index. Some people's faces

---

[2] Elwood A. Kretsinger, "An Experimental Study of Gross Bodily Movement as an Index to Audience Interest," *Speech Monographs,* vol. 14, November, 1952.

habitually fall into a smile or a frown in repose. A knitting of the brows could mean the listener is trying hard to understand you or is skeptical about what you are saying. A grin on someone's face could indicate approval, or simply that a gravy spot on your tie has been noticed; your listener may even have been thinking about something totally different that happened to seem amusing at that point. You should be aware of facial expressions, but recognize their limitations as measures of audience response.

DEALING WITH AN INATTENTIVE AUDIENCE

Suppose you find that despite your most careful preparation in terms of audience interest, your audience still isn't attentive? What can you do about it?

THE LISTENER'S STATE OF MIND

This is an aspect of audience attention over which you have no control. Even if you could find out all the things that were running through the minds of all the people in your audience, you couldn't do anything about them. Take just one grouchy-looking young man in the audience. As he left for school his landlady told him he was going to be evicted for back rent; he dented a fender on his father's car and the insurance had expired; and his biology teacher said he was failing the course. He is likely to have a lot more on his mind than your speech on the natural habitat of the red-headed woodpecker.

THE MOOD OF THE AUDIENCE

Sometimes there are external factors that affect the mood of the entire audience. In November, 1963, a few hours before the opening of a week-long national conference of a branch of the American Psychological Association, the news of President Kennedy's assassination reached the public. This was an audience vitally interested in the subject, who had traveled from all parts of the country just to attend. Most of the speakers tried to go on with the speeches they had planned because they didn't know what else to do, but it's unlikely that even they were paying much attention to what they said. You may never be confronted with a situation of this magnitude, but there will be times when it is pointless to try to compete with the mood of your audience.

ENVIRONMENTAL CONDITIONS

Here you have some control, although it may be limited. Before you begin speaking you should check to see that the physical situation is as favorable as possible. During your speech, however, you may have to deal with changes in the situation. For example, a room that was airy and comfortable when you began may become hot and stuffy after it has been full of people for a while. You might be able to have someone turn down the thermostat or open a window.

You may find yourself having to cope with unanticipated noise. In general, if the noise is louder than you are, don't try to compete with it. If it is going to be of short duration—say, a plane overhead—the best thing to do is just stop talking and wait it out. If someone is operating a jackhammer right outside the door, you will have to take more positive measures. Having someone close the door may help, but you might have to ask the worker if he can stop until you have finished.

DISTRACTIONS FROM THE AUDIENCE

Latecomers sometimes attract attention by their efforts to find seats. You may want to stop briefly to help them get settled, but try not to embarrass them by directing all eyes their way—and away from you. A more difficult problem to deal with is whispered conversations in the audience while you are speaking. To begin with, you are more likely to be distracted by this situation than your audience, since you are facing the whisperers, but the audience is facing you. If no one else is being distracted, it may be better to ignore the situation than to divert the attention of the rest of your audience. If you can catch the eye of the offenders discreetly, do so. In fact, if the people around them are being disturbed, they may do this themselves. If the interference is too great, you may have to do something about it. One thing to bear in mind, however, is that an admonishment of one member of the audience may affect your rapport with the rest. The members of an audience tend to identify more with each other than with the speaker, and a reprimand of one constitutes a threat to the entire group.

You will have to invent your own system for handling such situations, and often it will have to be done spontaneously. The more experience you acquire, the easier it will get. To a large extent, the success of what you do will depend on the rapport you have established with your audience.

THE QUALITY OF THE STIMULUS

This is the aspect of attention over which you have the most control. Audiences are in an essentially passive position, and as a result, their attention will be drawn to whatever stimulus is the strongest. If your material is interesting and you deliver it well, you should be able to compete against the stimulus of most minor distractions. The next time you are in an auditorium or a classroom check for yourself how intently the audience is listening. If you see a lot of heads turning when there is a slight noise or when someone gets up to leave, that's a sign that the stimulus provided by the speaker isn't strong enough to screen out small disruptions.

EMPHASIZING KEY POINTS

Speakers sometimes seem to have the idea that everything they say will be remembered. Classroom lecturers would certainly like to believe this is true, but the results of final examinations usually do not confirm the notion. Even when a speaker's delivery is effective and the audience is attentive, only a small percentage of the message will be retained. There are of course a number of variables: The importance of the information to the listeners, the extent to which they will be held responsible for the information, whether or not they are taking notes, and so on. But as a speaker, you must be realistic. Generally in a speech of twenty to thirty minutes in length, you will be able to make two or three key points at best. Think about it. If that is all the audience will be able to retain, what key points do you want them to remember, and how are you going to emphasize those points?

POSITION

The placement of a statement in the speech is one factor in audience retention. Although the evidence is subject to qualification, it appears that audiences are most likely to remember what you say first and what you say last. Plan your introduction and your conclusion carefully to take full advantage of these two vital areas of the speech. Audience attention is probably highest at the very beginning of the speech; it tapers off toward the middle and then picks up again when the audience senses that you are concluding. The points at which you have the greatest attention are the times to make your significant statements.

REPETITION

This appears to be the most effective mode of emphasis. The studies indicate that a statement repeated three to five times in a speech is generally remembered. This may be a bit too much in a short speech, but it does give you some idea. Repetition may be either *concentrated* or *distributed.* If you were using concentrated repetition you might repeat your statement in different words:

> The population of the world will double in the next thirty years. There will be twice as many people on our planet in the year 2010.

Or you might restate it in exactly the same words, perhaps with different inflection. If you distribute your repetition at different points in the speech, the impact is greater if you restate it in the same words, with strong vocal emphasis.

Look at the use of restatement in these memorable words by Winston Churchill:

> We shall defend our island, whatever the cost may be. We shall fight on the beaches. We shall fight on the landing grounds. We shall fight in the fields and in the streets, and we shall fight in the hills. We shall never surrender.

THE POINTER PHRASE

One exceedingly effective way to emphasize an important statement is simply to announce that you are about to make an important statement. Consider your own reaction when an instructor says

> Now, this is important and will probably be included on the final examination.

If you can, include the reason the following point is important:

> *One point stands out, and this is something that will affect us all within our own lifetime. Unless we can change the present trend, the population of the world will double in the next thirty years.*

Be sure, however, that the statement you are pointing to is truly significant, and that is stated in such a way that it can be remembered easily.

ORATORICAL EMPHASIS

The methods we have discussed so far apply to written statements as well as to spoken ones. However, there are some modes of emphasis that are available only to a speaker. They include such things as dramatic pauses, changes in vocal inflection and volume, and movement and gesture. As a speaker you have access not only to verbal communication, but to all the methods of nonverbal communication as well. You might consider such devices a bit "hammy," but they are the same things you would do spontaneously in any other situation. Employing them purposely does not make them less legitimate as a means of communication as long as your purpose itself is a legitimate one.

If you accept the contention that people can believe a falsehood as easily as they can believe a truth, it follows that the message they receive depends to a large extent on the skill of the speaker. Truth and justice are not self-evident. The only way they can prevail is if they are advocated by honest and just men and women who are effective in their communication. Sixteen hundred years ago St. Augustine wrote:

> *Who will dare to say that truth in the person of its defenders is to take its stand unarmed against falsehood? . . . Are those who are trying to persuade men of what is false to know how to introduce their subject, so as to put the hearer into a friendly, or attentive, or teachable frame of mind, while the defenders of the truth shall be ignorant of that art? That the former are to tell their falsehoods briefly, clearly, and plausibly, while the latter shall tell the truth in such a way that is tedious to listen to, hard to understand, and, in fine,*

not easy to believe . . . . Who is such a fool as to think this wisdom?[3]

QUESTIONS FOR DISCUSSION

1 How reliably can you judge a person's reaction by the look on his or her face? Which of the covert responses would you say was the most reliable indication?

2 If you found after you began to speak that your audience was not interested in what you were saying, what would you do about it?

3 What are some of the ways in which a speaker can deal with distractions in the audience? What methods do you think might be effective for you? How would you deal with a deliberate heckler?

4 Would you consider it ethical to stimulate an audience by planting people to applaud? Where would you draw the line between legitimate persuasion and manipulation?

5 Can an intelligent audience always pick out the important points of any speech? What purpose does oratorical emphasis serve?

SUGGESTED ACTIVITIES

1 Divide the class into two groups, A and B. In two to three minutes have someone from A relate something to someone from B. It could be a narrative of a personal experience, an explanation of a process, or an expression of an opinion. The person from B must listen without asking questions or taking notes and then repeat to the class what the person from A said. Afterward check with the latter to see if that was what was meant.

[3] *On Christian Doctrine*, book IV, chap. 2, trans. J. F. Shaw, Great Books of the Western World, vol. 18, William Benton, Publisher, Chicago, 1952.

2 As an impromptu exercise have one person stand in front of the class audience and make a single statement about a topic she or he wishes to discuss. Other people in the class then ask questions about it. Evaluate the questions as well as the speaker's response. Were they really questions? Were they clearly stated? Were they designed to get information? Was the speaker in control of the situation? Did the speaker recognize everyone who had a question? Were the speaker's responses direct and succinct?

8

UNDERSTANDING THE AUDIENCE

In public speaking we say that our purpose is to *deliver* a message to an audience. But can we deliver a message in the same way that we can deliver a package? Does it always come neatly wrapped and securely tied? And will the contents be perceived by the receiver in the same way as they are viewed by the sender? Delivering a speech is far more complex than delivering a package, and the complexities are multiplied as the size of the audience increases.

Sometimes speakers forget that an audience is composed of individuals each with a unique set of personal experiences that will affect the way the message is received

THE AUDIENCE IS PLURAL

The word "audience" is one that might give us some trouble because it can be used in reference to one person or to many. Normally we think of a gathering of people listening to one or more speakers, but the grammar of our language tends to distort the reality of our meaning. "Audience" is a collective noun and is commonly used with a singular verb—we say, "The audience is . . . . " The implication here is that it will respond as one person, and such is not always the case. When we say, "The audience liked the speech," we are really saying that our observation was that most of the people responded favorably. It is necessary for us to understand that each individual in the audience will hear a different message and will respond in a different way. All of the messages may be substantially different from what the speaker actually intended. The discrepancy occurs because a message is monitored within the framework of the individual's perceived reality. Each will be receiving what he or she regards as important, rejecting that which is unacceptable, disregarding what is not comprehensible, and perhaps even modifying some of the speaker's most cherished points. In other words, the members of an audience do not listen to what *the speaker says;* they listen to what *they hear.*

Public speaking has significant disadvantages over conversational communication. In conversation you can make one point at a time and get a reaction to it before you go on to the next one. But this procedure would encumber the public speaking mode by taking too much time and by diverting the speaker away from a planned organizational pattern. The public speaker using effective techniques can communicate a large amount of information to a great number of people in a short period of time. But this advantage is gained only when speakers do their homework and are well-prepared.

Try to understand the orientation of the audience you plan to address, and see if the message you want to send is one that they are willing to hear. This advice does not imply that you must appease and pamper your audience, but it does mean you will be more successful if you are able to anticipate possible roadblocks to your communication. If the audience stops listening, you might just as well stop talking.

STEPPING INTO THE LISTENER'S SHOES

Preparation for your talk begins immediately after you accept an invitation to speak. Once you have made the commitment there is a tendency to begin thinking in terms of the message you are going to send. But if, instead, you start thinking of yourself as someone in the audience rather than the speaker on the platform, you may get some insight into gaining and maintaining the attention of the people to whom you are going to speak.

1   You know, for example, that when you come to hear someone speak, you bring with you a multitude of thoughts which are not related either to speaker or topic. Those thoughts may be far more vital to you than what the speaker is saying, and in spite of your efforts to focus on the words of the speaker, you begin ruminating on other matters. From this experience of your own you can draw the first conclusion in understanding the audience: The individual's mind tends to wander—the speaker must compete for attention with the other concerns important in the listener's life.

2   Again, using yourself as an example, you know that not all topics are of interest to you. You pay close attention when the matter is important and touches your life in some way, but your attention drifts off if the subject is not relevant to you. You "tune out" the speaker who expects you to generate your own motivation whether you are interested or not. Conclusion number two, then, is that the speaker must not assume that the audience has a built-in interest in his or her topic. The motivation must be created.

3   Even if you (as a member of the audience) like the topic, you might get a negative impression of the speaker that will interfere with the focus of your attention. Your rejection of the speaker may be based upon his or her mannerisms or style of delivery. Or you may have certain prejudices that you are unable to control regarding age, sex, race, or nationality. The reasons for your attitude may be more emotional than rational, but either way you find that your listening is impaired. The third point of analysis is that a speaker cannot expect the audience to be nonjudgmental about personal

mannerisms and style, or even about attributes over which he or she has no control.

4   If the topic is one that interests you and the speaker is someone whom you can accept, your attention is still not guaranteed. You will listen only as long as the speaker is saying something interesting. Perhaps you have had the experience of going to a lecture with excitement and anticipation to hear something about a topic of great concern to you. The subject itself may have gained your attention, but the speaker failed to develop it in an engaging fashion and your thoughts probably wandered. The fourth point of analysis is that the examples and supporting materials the speaker selects are of paramount importance in maintaining audience attention.

5   Your interest will be held only as long as you are able to understand what the speaker is saying. If the language is over your head, you will probably do one of two things: either guess at the speaker's meaning or tune out altogether. On the other hand, if the language is beneath you— if the speaker is downgrading your intelligence by using a childish vocabulary—your attitude toward the speaker may well become strongly negative. Point five is that choice of words and use of language can either enhance or impede listening.

6   One of the most severe inhibitors of communication is insufficient volume. Have you ever gone to a lecture and had to strain to hear the speaker? How long are you able to pay attention when the voice is barely audible? Probably not long. If you can't hear, you can't listen. The sixth point is that a speaker must be heard, and the volume of the speech must be sufficient to override distracting noises.

7   In analyzing your own receptivity ask yourself the question, "How long am I able to listen?" The answer to that may give you some insight into the attention span of most audiences. There are, of course, a number of variable factors, but studies have shown that listening begins to drop off after the first twenty minutes. At the end of an hour the listening curve drops very sharply. Point number seven in audience analysis is that the overextended speech is difficult to listen to—that

for maximum effectiveness the speaker should compress the speech into the shortest possible time frame.

8 Your comfort as a listener will also have an influence upon your attention. There are an infinite number of variables that might fall into this category: The chair you are sitting in, the number of people in the room, the temperature and ventilation, the ambient noises, the surrounding furnishings, the wall hangings, the weather conditions—all could have an effect upon your comfort and consequently upon your ability to listen. Usually a comfortable environment will enhance audience receptiveness, but there is the possibility that too much comfort will cause people to fall asleep. The eighth point of analysis is that the speaker must give consideration to the external conditions of the audience's environment.

FILLING THE LISTENERS' NEEDS

The eight points of analysis will give you an idea of what you have to do as a speaker. First of all, accept the fact that there are other things going on in the minds of your listeners and that you will have to rely upon your rhetorical skills to gain and hold their attention. Select a subject that can be linked to the interests of the audience. You can do this by choosing references and examples that are relevant to their experience. Try to estimate how much your audience already knows about the subject and don't go into much depth if their knowledge is limited. You will have little success, for example, explaining the finer points of opera to an audience familiar only with popular music. But you would be able to hold attention with unusual stories about occurrences at performances, or devices used behind the scenes for special effects.

DEALING WITH A PREJUDICED AUDIENCE

Prejudice against a speaker is a factor that students often regard as the most disturbing of all. What do you do when members of an audience have negative feelings about your age, sex, race, or nationality? The best you can do is to demonstrate that you are one person who is not consistent with their stereotype. Try to figure out, if you can, what preconceived notions about your character or personality might prevail in their minds. Some typical stereotypes are that old people are self-serving, reactionary, and rigid in their thinking; women are ill-informed, flighty, and disorganized; Third World people are violent and irresponsible. If you are an older person who can advance modern and progressive ideas or a woman who can speak intelligently and in a well-organized fashion or a Third World person who can advocate reasonable and responsible action, you may not only win over your audience, but take a big step toward dispelling prejudicial attitudes. Your age, sex, race, and nationality are factors that will have an effect upon your communication, but they are certainly not the only factors. There is no need to feel defeated if you find yourself facing a prejudiced audience, nor is there need for you to return the prejudice that has been directed toward you.

There was a time when no candidate could win an election in Boston who didn't have an Irish name, and when most people would not even listen to a man who had long hair or black skin. Convictions based on prejudice are often deep-seated—and just as often they are hidden. People do not like to think that they are prejudiced. They prefer to see themselves as rational beings who base their judgments on facts. As a result they are often not aware themselves of the biases that influence their acceptance or rejection of a speaker's ideas.

Politicians as a group are acutely aware of this factor in their audiences. One of the techniques they have used to cut across racial and cultural boundaries is to find some means of linking themselves to the group they are addressing, some area in which the audience can identify with them as "one of their own kind." The fact that this has sometimes been done with little regard for integrity doesn't invalidate the technique itself as an effective means of overcoming what can be a serious barrier to communication. Whether we like it or not, prejudices do exist, and the speaker who fails to take them into consideration is unable to deal with them. The unscrupulous may take advantage of them; the sincere will treat them honestly; but only the naïve will ignore them.

OVERCOMING YOUR OWN WEAKNESSES

Public speaking is an art, not a science. Therefore, it is not necessary to conform to a rigid model in order to achieve success. Most people can learn to speak effectively, and almost any personal deficiency can be overcome. What's more, there are ways to compensate for weaknesses that cannot be overcome. While some speakers have the ability to make an effective emotional appeal, others may not feel comfortable attempting it. These speakers too, however, can hold and influence their audiences by presenting information in an interesting and logical fashion. Finding information and organizing it effectively is a skill that can be learned by anyone who has the motivation to do so. It is also possible for anyone to learn such other skills as gaining the attention of the audience early in the speech, holding it with clearly stated main ideas, developing those ideas with concrete examples, and concluding the speech before it gets tiresome. The speaker whose voice is not strong does not have to give up on public speaking. One alternative is to speak to smaller groups; another is to use a public-address system; a third is to study vocal technique and diction and learn to project the voice.

PREPARING TO MEET THE AUDIENCE

Suppose you have been invited by one of the local service clubs to speak at its weekly luncheon meeting. The first thing you do is accept—that's important because willingness is an essential ingredient in this whole process. Next, find out from the person who invited you as much as you can about the audience and the total environment. You will want to know the size of the group, and whether it is a formal or informal occasion. If the group is large and rather formal, you may need a public-address system. Be sure to find out how long you are expected to speak and if there will be a question period afterward. You should also know if there are going to be other speakers on the program, and if so, what their topics will be. If you plan to use visual aids, find out what facilities are available. You may need an easel for charts, a chalkboard, a projector and screen, or a pointer. These are not generally provided unless you request them.

Success in public speaking means giving attention to as many variables as you can control. Knowing that the physical environment plays a part in determining the audience's listening behavior, you may wish to check the room prior to the time you speak to see that there is adequate seating and ventilation, and that there is a minimum of distracting influences.

The most important consideration, however, is that your speech itself meet the needs and expectations of the audience. Find out why you have been asked to speak. Were you picked because your audience wants information on a particular topic? Or do they want you in particular as a speaker, regardless of your topic? A speaker who has developed a reputation in a community may often be invited to talk on any subject of his or her choice. Is this a group that prefers to steer clear of controversial matters, or do they want to hear your views on an issue of interest to them? It is not courteous to take advantage of a speaking situation to push some pet cause unless you have been specifically invited to do so. If you are asked to give an informative speech, be sure that you do just that.

Before you even begin preparing your speech you will have to give thought to the audience you are going to address. In order to communicate with them effectively there are a number of factors you are going to have to take into consideration.

WILL THE AUDIENCE BE INTERESTED?

Let's say that you have been asked to give an expository speech on the local community college because this is an area in which you are informed. Your topic has been specified, but it's still a pretty broad one. In organizing your material you will have to focus on the points that are most relevant to the people you are talking to—and to do this you have to know something about them.

Suppose, for instance, that the club has invited a group of high school students to hear you. In this case you might orient your remarks to those who are considering enrollment in the college. You could talk about the curriculum and the courses that are offered, or about social activities and athletics—in short, the aspects that would be of interest to incoming students. What if you were addressing the business executives of the community, the ones who pay the taxes that supports the college? Here your approach would be slightly different. You might discuss the financing of the college and point out what the taxpayers are getting for their money—say, the cultural activities the college provides for the community. If your audience were made up of prospective teachers planning their careers, you could discuss some aspects of teaching at the community college level. You might be able to give them some idea of the general academic atmosphere, the nature of the student body, and what the students expect from the faculty. These are just three examples of entirely different speeches in the same subject area, each designed for the interests of a specific audience.

The more you can learn about the audience the more effective you will be able to be in planning your speech. Groups that meet on a regular basis almost always have some common denominator. For example, they may all be members of a particular business or profession. Salespeople, accountants, technical writers often have their own associations, and the name of the group may or may not give you a clue. An organization called the High Notes may have a membership of musicians, but it might also be airplane pilots. Find out from the chairperson. . . . And if the name does pertain to music, you would still need to know what kind. It is important for you to know because you don't want to give a speech to an audience on a subject that they know more about than you. Nor would you want to give a speech that is completely irrelevant to their interests. To musicians who play classical music, you may want to talk about methods of publicizing musical events, or what other communities have done to organize chamber music groups. If you are an expert in your field you can talk to other experts, but if you are not, the best plan is to select a topic you do know something about and adapt it to the interests of your audience.

If your speech is one of a series, find out what ideas were advanced in earlier speeches so that you can make specific references to them. Try to work into your speech some activities that are of particular concern to your audience. If the speech is on the techniques of conducting a group discussion, ask whether any group discussions are planned for later programs. If so, select examples that your audience can apply in the actual situations that will confront them. Real examples are best, but hypothetical ones will serve.

The important thing is to anticipate as well as you can what kind of information your audience will want to have. It is possible, of course, to make some adjustments after you start talking, but this is difficult to do unless you are very experienced. For now, the best procedure is to plan your speech as well as you can, and then give it the way you planned it.

WILL THE AUDIENCE UNDERSTAND YOU?

You will never know for sure whether the audience receives the message the same way you intended it. The only way to find out would be for you to ask each individual member of the audience to paraphrase what he or she thinks you have said. Not only is this impractical, it is unreliable; you may not clearly understand the paraphrase. It is important to remember that the *message is the message received.* People may completely misconstrue what you meant, but whatever they thought they heard is the way it *actually is* for them. There are many reasons why your message may not be understood; let's look at just a few of them.

LANGUAGE

When we think of barriers to communication, language is one of the first things that comes to mind. Obviously two people must understand the same language in order to communicate at an abstract level. But even within the same language, dialects, accents, verbal expressions, and even grammatical construction vary considerably. To an American a thick Scottish brogue can sound like a foreign language.

Slang expressions are common in every language. They are useful because they provide symbolization for concepts, attitudes, and feelings that cannot adequately be expressed by a standard lexicon. Slang expressions also serve the purpose of unifying members of a subculture. They have the same effect as the secret passwords you used to make up when you were a kid. They provide a means of identifying those people who share common interests and attitudes. The language of the drug culture is full of slang because the intent of those who speak it is to provide insulation from the outside world. Remember that while slang brings together those who understand the language, it shuts out those who do not. While colloquial expressions may add spice to your message, they also tend to obscure it. Slang is more volatile than standard English; it changes meaning more rapidly. Sometimes members of the older generation have trouble understanding their offspring, not because the words are unknown, but because they are used in an unfamiliar way. "Stoned," "joint," and "busted" are all expressions that had different meanings a generation ago.

ATTITUDES

Communication breakdowns may occur because one person doesn't understand another's attitude. It is not only a language barrier that separates members of two subcultures, but their perspective on life as well. It is entirely possible for you to learn all the slang expressions used by a particular group and still not share their frame of reference. If you are Caucasian, you may be able to speak the language of the black culture, but you will never know how the world looks to its members. Someone raised in Harlem or Watts has a very different attitude toward words such as "authority," than one brought up in white-middle-class suburbia. A prime example of attitudinal differences is that which revolves around the concept of "law and order." Usually the people who claim to be for it are referring to violations such as armed robbery and burglary. Their attitudes do not permit them to include flagrant abuses of public property, income-tax evasion, and political corruption.

Determining audience attitude toward the topic is not an easy task. Even if you ask people how they feel, you can't rely on their answers. Sometimes they will be unwilling to tell you, but often they will not really know themselves. People are concerned about their self-image and will go to any length to preserve it. A person with a self-image of being intelligent and cultured might profess to like opera, but you may be sadly disappointed in his or her actual response to a speech on this topic.

It is not my intention to make value judgments about language or attitudes, only to say that they are factors to be considered in audience analysis. Regardless of how valuable your message may be, you will alienate yourself if you do not have the perception and sensitivity to know the language level or attitudinal posture of your audience.

EDUCATIONAL LEVEL

It might be a bit difficult to determine the educational level of your audience, but you should try to estimate it. This will be an important factor in determining the level of your vocabulary and the complexity of your sentence structure. It is just as bad to talk down to an audience as it is to talk over their heads. The formal education of your audience will also influence the examples you use. Literary and historical allusions can lend color and interest to your speech, but only if your audience understands and appreciates them. The exploits of Paul Bunyan or Don Quixote will probably be familiar to most people, but a reference to Hecuba may be recognized by only a very specialized audience. Don't make the mistake of assuming, however, that a lack of formal education is necessarily an indication of ignorance. Some very well-read people have never gotten past high school—and conversely, many college graduates haven't opened a book since receiving their degrees.

WILL THE AUDIENCE ACCEPT WHAT YOU SAY?

Even if you have planned a speech that your audience will understand, the attitudes and opinions they already hold will influence both the message they receive and their willingness to accept what you tell them. It is necessary for you to know as much as you can about the *demographics* of your audience. The more information you have about your listeners' age, sex, occupation, income level, political and religious affiliations, race, nationality, and so on, the better prepared you will be in anticipating the acceptability of your message. Your analysis for a public-speaking occasion is not much different from that which you make in less formal situations. Colburn and Weinberg tell us that, "People use demographic analysis to assess groups in many everyday situations, whether they realize it or not . . . Through trial and error, most people become quite expert in drawing meaningful conclusions about groups of people based upon the demographic characteristics of those groups. These conclusions . . . enable an individual to develop a mental set that prepares him or her to react in a prescribed way."[1] As a speaker, you may choose to behave in a way that is contrary to the norms of the group you are addressing, but when you do so you must be aware of the risk of having your ideas rejected.

POLITICAL SENTIMENTS

In the past several years it has become increasingly difficult to predict the response of political organizations. There are considerably more registered Democrats than Republicans in this coun-

[1] C. William Colburn and Sanford B. Weinberg, "An Orientation to Listening and Audience Analysis", *Modcom: Modules in Speech Communication*, Science Research Associates, Inc., Chicago, 1976, p. 24.

try, and yet since 1950 the Republicans have occupied the White House longer than the Democrats. Even though voters express a preference for a political party they apparently do not feel constrained to follow the party line. This means that it's quite possible for a speaker to advocate the election of a candidate even though the audience is composed largely of people who support the opposing party. Usually the speaker can expect that the audience will listen and consider what is said, even if there is no general concurrence. And there is always the possibility of winning some support. The fact that a large portion of American voters do not remain loyal to their party has both advantages and disadvantages. One of the main reasons for this phenomenon is that political platforms consist of many planks, and people tend to be more committed to issues than to candidates. While you may get a polite response from those who disagree with you about a political party, you may get a hostile response from those who oppose you on an issue about which they have strong convictions. It behooves you to make some inquiries about your audience if you are to speak on an issue that is highly controversial.

Sometimes political leanings can be estimated from occupational or group associations. For example, you can generally assume that union members will be opposed to restrictions on strikes, teachers will favor aid-to-education programs, business executives will support corporate tax reductions, police officers will be critical of strict arrest procedures, and so on. The more committed an organization is to a cause, the more critical the listeners will be of a speaker who opposes their viewpoint. For example, you should recognize the risk of attacking the Equal Rights Amendment when speaking to the National Organization of Women, or what may happen when you suggest gun registration to the National Rifle Association.

RELIGIOUS BELIEFS

It isn't likely that you will be asking any members of the audience to change their religion, but if you are addressing a group with specific religious convictions you had better know what those convictions are. They would certainly be a factor, for example, if you were speaking on fluoridation of water to an audience of Christian Scientists, or on the preparation of roast suckling pig to an audience of Orthodox Jews, or on the advantages of tub baths over showers to an audience of Moslems. In this kind of situation you are dealing not with just one idea, but with an entire set of values and beliefs which may be fundamental to your listeners' way of life. Dealing with religious issues is extremely difficult and requires that you be realistic in your expectations of the audience response. If your subject is public funding for abortion, you will have little chance of winning the approval of the Roman Catholics in the audience. You will either have to do without their support, or change your thesis. You might be more successful with a speech calling for the use of public funds to provide counseling for pregnant women.

In the process of audience analysis we must be careful not to stereotype and assume that all people who subscribe to a particular religion will react to an issue in the same way. John F. Kennedy, for example, a Roman Catholic, was opposed to the use of federal funds for parochial schools. We can find many other cases in these times when theological principles so often enter into social and political problems. The right of homosexuals to teach in public schools has come up squarely against some religious doctrines, and the fact that it has does not mean the issue should be avoided. There are many controversies, even within particular denominations, where both sides are supported by people of goodwill who see different paths to the same end. Topics such as divorce, feminism, capital punishment, euthanasia, prayers in school, abortion, and sex education are all issues which involve religious principles.

RESPECT FOR THE AUDIENCE

Keep in mind that your function in a public-speaking situation is to provide an audience with a message that will be valuable to them. You are on the platform for their benefit, not for your own. You may be getting certain rewards from the experience—it may be gratifying and fulfilling—but basically your purpose is to give something to the listeners that they will be able to remember and use in some way in their own lives. They may or may not accept the ideas you want them to accept. If they do, you have achieved your objective and you can take satisfaction from that. If they don't, you must accept that also. There is no way you can force your message upon them. If there is opposition to what you say, you can do your best to overcome it, but finally you must respect the right of any audience to believe what they want to believe. You may experience anger and frustration when you are convinced that you are right and they are wrong, but you have nothing to gain by directing your anger at the listeners. If on any occasion you are tempted to do that, stop and consider: What is your goal? Do you really want them to accept your message, or do you want the satisfaction of "blowing off steam"? There is a good chance that the resistance might be coming from just a few individuals in the audience. If that's the case, you can afford to lose them. Be satisfied if you have won over even a few. Making an overzealous attack upon an audience may result in alienating not only those who oppose you, but the rest as well.

QUESTIONS FOR DISCUSSION

1 Do you think that slanting your material to a particular audience is dishonest? Under what circumstances is it advantageous to the audience?

2 Do you think age is the primary factor in the generation gap? You have probably heard some men say, "I'll never understand women." Why do you think men and women have trouble communicating with each other?

3 Would you say that people are more open-minded about political issues than about religious issues? Can you think of any situations in which the reverse might be true?

4 Is it a compromise of principle for a speaker to base an argument on some ground other than the one he or she considers the primary issue? Would you say that this was an evasion of the issue? Do you think it is a compromise of principle for speakers to aim for anything less than complete acceptance of their ideas?

5 Are there any differences in the ways a speaker might deal with open prejudice and hidden prejudice? Do you often judge people's attitudes by their regional accents?

6 If a speaker can expect no more than to be heard out, is there any point in speaking at all?

SUGGESTED ACTIVITIES

1 Prepare a statistical profile of your class. Use the following
   form: Age _____ Sex _____
   Marital status _____
   Children _____
   Political affiliation: Republican _____
                         Democrat _____
                         Other _____
   Religious affiliation: Protestant _____
                         Catholic _____
                         Other _____
   Working full time _____
   Working part time _____
   Number of hours _____
   Financial support: Self _____
                      Parents _____
                      VA _____
                      Welfare _____
                      Other _____
   Years of college _____
   Did you vote in the last election? _____

2 On the basis of the information received from the above
   form, prepare a campaign speech as though you were running for a state office. Explain your stand on controversial
   issues; tell how you would vote on pending legislation. Have
   three people campaign for the same office. After the three
   speeches, take a vote.

9

RECEIVING
THE MESSAGE

In Aristotle's model we have seen that in order for communication to take place there must be an audience as well as a message and a speaker. Often what *appears* to be communication is nothing more than a group of people in the same room exchanging sounds. The presence of an audience is not necessarily assurance that communication is taking place. There is a difference between *hearing* sounds and *listening* to a message. Perhaps you have been to cocktail parties or casual social gatherings where people are talking but are not really communicating. Such a condition might be referred to as *non-listening,* and it happens more than we would like to think. As a student of the communication process you need to look at your listening behavior as well as your speaking ability.

THE IMPORTANCE OF LISTENING

For two thousand years speech pedagogy focused upon the message and the speaker. Listening was taken for granted and regarded as a function that would come about automatically if the message were well presented. In other words, the unspoken premise was that the responsibility for communication rested primarily upon the sender, and if the idea did not get across it was because the speaker did not make it clear. Not until the middle of the twentieth century did we begin to view listening as a skill and as active rather than passive behavior.

One of the early studies was conducted by Ralph Nichols who provided us with some important evidence.[1] First of all, he pointed out that most of our communication time is spent in listening—over 60 percent. The rest is divided among talking, reading, and writing. But prior to 1950 there was no effort to teach people to listen. Even today listening is seldom taught in schools and often only casually mentioned even in communication courses. The need is obviously great because Nichols points out that immediately after listening to a ten-minute presentation the average listener is able to remember less than half of it.[2] And two days later, that figure drops to 25 percent.

Sylvia Porter, nationally syndicated financial columnist, regards effective listening as being a vital cog in the wheels of industry. "With 100 million workers in our nation," she says, "a simple ten dollar listening mistake by each would cost business a billion dollars."[3] She quotes the chief executive of the Sperry Corporation as saying, "Poor listening is one of the most significant problems facing business today. Business relies on its communications system, and when it breaks down, mistakes can be very costly. Corporations pay for their mistakes in lower profits,

---

[1] Ralph Nichols, *Are You Listening?*, McGraw-Hill, New York, 1957.

[2] Ibid.

[3] Sylvia Porter, "Are you Listening? Really Hearing," *San Francisco Chronicle*, Nov. 6, 1979.

while consumers pay in higher prices." This evidence may make you wonder about your own listening habits and cause you to ask yourself, "How can I improve my listening so that I can comprehend and retain more information?"

LISTENING SITUATIONS

If we were to examine closely the communicating we do every day, we would probably find that much of it is purely for the sake of making contact with another human being. When we talk to our friends and family we are motivated by something other than just the need to give and receive information. We want to nurture the relationship. The content of what we say is often less important than the process of communicating. Think of an enjoyable conversation you have recently had with a close friend. How much of the content do you remember? Perhaps not much. But th, t does not negate the value of the conversation. Relating to people is a fulfilling experience even when only a small percentage of the message is retained.

There are other kinds of listening situations in which the content may not be the most important factor. Often we listen purely for the sake of appreciating the sounds. We go to a concert to enjoy the music rather than to expand our knowledge. Sometimes we are moved by a speaker because an emotional feeling has been stirred—not through the content of the message, but by the rhythm, the tone, and the harmony of the words.

Some listening that we do is for the purpose of being uplifted and inspired, or having our cherished convictions reinforced. We may not learn anything that we did not already know, but we feel good about the experience and believe that the time was well spent.

LISTENING FOR CONTENT

There are times, however, when the content of the message is important, and the receiver needs to apply listening skills. It is necessary first of all to learn to identify the various kinds of communication situations, and apply the listening skills that are most appropriate.

EMPATHIC LISTENING

You probably have noticed that you listen better on some occasions than you do on others. The chances are that you do not consciously identify the variables determining the quality of your listening, and certainly there are more than we could possibly list. Some broad categories might include the following:

Your physical condition   If you are tired or sick, your listening ability may not be what it should be.

The listening environment   The temperature of the room, the seating arrangements, outside distractions, and a multitude of related factors will affect your listening.

The importance of the message   How well you listen certainly will be affected by the position that the information occupies on your list of priorities.

Your relationship with the speaker   The attitude you have toward the sender of the message may enhance or inhibit your listening ability.

Much of our listening is done when only the *content* is important. In other words, we do not need to understand the *person*, we only need to understand the message. *Empathic* listening, on the other hand is that which involves us in the total communication complex. We want to become fully aware of whatever it is that the sender is experiencing. Listening is best when we are physically alert, when the environment is favorable, when the message has a high priority, and when our relationship with the sender is conducive. Charles Kelly tells us that "empathic listening occurs when the person participates in the spirit or feeling of his environment as a communication receiver."[4] This may be the same as saying that good listening means that the receiver must be *motivated* to listen. Kelly says, "It is likely that

---

[4] "Empathic Listening" by Charles M. Kelly, from *Speech Communication: a Basic Anthology*, Ronald L. Appelbaum and Owen O. Jensen, and Richard Carroll, Macmillan, New York, 1975, p. 116.

most communication problems arise either because of participant inattention (poor motivation) or because of lack of general mental ability—not because of anything that can be called 'listening ability'."[5]

Common practice is to listen *judgmentally* rather than empathically. When we do this, we are contaminating the message with values of our own that were not intended by the sender. In other words we tend to edit what we hear—adding, subtracting, and distorting portions of the message. "Empathic listening is difficult because we usually need to do it when our emotions are involved. Empathic listening is most needed when emotional involvement is highest. But the very emotion we bring to the situation interferes with the effort to see things as someone else does."[6]

The concept of empathic listening was developed by Carl Rogers in his book, *On Becoming a Person*. He says, " . . . the major barrier to mutual interpersonal communication is our very natural tendency to judge, to evelate, to approve or disapprove, the statement of the other person."[7] He suggests the following experiment: "The next time you get into an argument with your wife, or your friend, or with a small group of friends, stop the discussion for a moment and institute this rule. 'Each person can speak up for himself only *after* he has first restated the ideas and feelings of the previous speaker accurately, and to that speaker's satisfaction.'[7] "

ACTIVE LISTENING

Active listening is based upon the contention that the feedback you provide as a listener has an effect upon the sender of the message. We all know this to be true, that we are much more inclined to talk to people whom we perceive to be listening. If they nod and comment from time to time about what we are saying, we are encouraged to pursue the topic in more detail. If we receive no response, or an unfavorable reply, we tend to back off from what we are saying.

[5] Ibid., p. 120.

[6] Anita Taylor et al., *Communicating*, Prentice-Hall, Englewood Cliffs, N.J., 1977, p. 153.

[7] Carl Rogers, *On Becoming a Person*, Houghton-Mifflin, Boston, 1961, pp. 330-332.

Psychologists have known for some time that listening is good therapy. People with emotional problems often find they are able to discover their own solutions if they can just talk about them to someone who will listen and reflect back to them what it is that they are saying. The method is to tell the sender of the message what it is that has been heard. The sender can then verify if that is what was meant, and in doing so, sort out his or her own feelings and acquire fresh insight. Obviously, active listening is not something you want to do all the time or in all communication situations. It is a skill reserved for rather specific occasions: (1) When the receiver wants to encourage the sender to pursue the topic; (2) When both the sender and the receiver want to make sure the message has been received accurately; and (3) When the sender is exploring ideas in his own head and wants to hear how they sound. Active listening skills are by no means the exclusive property of professional psychologists. They can be learned by anyone and applied effectively in any kind of intimate or helping relationship.

RETENTIVE LISTENING

In a course on interpersonal communication, active listening is a subject that would be pursued and developed in considerable detail. In a course on public speaking, however, we are primarily concerned with listening for retention. Let's look at the listener's responsibility to comprehend and retain what is being said. The primary reason for improving listening skills is to expand the receiver's fund of knowledge—to provide new ideas and new information. It may be that you will be called upon to interpret information and answer questions about it as you would in a classroom setting. You may have to understand directions and act upon them, or comprehend an explanation and recall it at a later time. It may be that you want to assimilate the information for your own edification and use. There are several steps you can take to improve your listening efficiency:

1   *Tune in at the start of the message.* One of the most common weaknesses in listening is the failure to hear the beginning portion of a statement. A normal pattern for speakers (as well as writers) is to specify the names of persons, places, or things at the beginning of a message and then use pronouns after that. If you miss the noun at the start, you may not understand the message at all.

2 *Listen for the main idea.* Sometimes speakers don't always get to the point right away. In conversation you can ask a person to clarify, but when listening to a speaker on the platform you can only interpret as best as you can. You may find that making your own tentative paraphrase is a useful method of filing the speaker's meaning in your mind, as long as you are aware that such interpretation is subject to revision if a different idea emerges. In any case, grasping the main idea provides a framework to which you can attach the specific details.

3 *Listen for details.* Effective listeners are those who are able to comprehend and retain not just the main idea, but the particular details. By details we mean the names of people, places, and things along with quotations, facts, statistics, instances, case histories, references, and literary and historic allusions. First you must be able to perceive the detail and allow it to enter your conscious mind; next, you must form an image of it either symbolically or nonsymbolically so that it can be filed in your mind; then you have to relate it to something so that it has significance; and finally, you must be able to retrieve it when you need to. All of that must be done in the time that it takes for the speaker to say it, so that you don't miss the next detail that follows.

4 *Listen for new information.* All too frequently we tend to listen to that which we already know and ignore the new information. We find it easy to go over familiar ground and have old ideas reinforced, but more difficult to absorb new material. The first step is to learn to identify the new information and perceive that it is different from that which is already known. Next, you must find a new place for it in your mental filing system, and establish a method of retrieval. Try if you can to relate the new information to something you already know; then, at your first opportunity use it in the context of your own thinking. Once you have articulated the material yourself, it becomes part of your own knowledge.

5 *Suspend judgment.* Listening is often hampered by judgmental attitudes. In other words, there is a common tendency for people to hear only what they *want* to hear. Recognize that your value structure plays an important role in your listening habits. If what is said is contrary to what you believe, you may shut out the message completely. Ideas pertaining to particular political, religious, or moral persuasions are frequently subject to judgmental selectivity in listening. The Protestant may be unwilling to hear anything favorable about Catholics, the Democrat may not listen to anything positive about Republicans, and so on. Dealing with this impediment depends upon your ability to let go of preconceived notions, and to recognize that failure to listen is more damaging to the receiver than to the sender.

6 *Focus upon the incoming message rather than your reply.* As a member of the audience you would probably not be called upon to make a response to what the speaker has said. But in an interview situation, a symposium, panel discussion, debate, or even social conversation you know you are going to be expected to make a reply. It is easy to fall into the trap of mentally phrasing the response you want to make rather than listening to what the other person is saying. Being aware of this difficulty is one thing, but overcoming it is something else. The experience you get in public speaking will be helpful because you will learn to rely upon spontaneity in answering, leaving your mind free to listen.

CRITICAL LISTENING

The principles pertaining to retentive listening also apply to critical listening. The prime requisite of listening for content is to comprehend and retain the ideas and information of the speaker. Critical listening goes one step further and calls for interpretation, evaluation, and response. The listener must do more than just absorb the information; he or she must also be prepared to analyze it and determine if the message is to be accepted, rejected, modified, or refuted. Critical listening is especially important in a political setting. Your understanding and analysis of what is being said by a candidate for office is vital to the functioning of a democracy. Year after year public officials are returned to office by voters who may have heard the voices of the candidates but did not listen critically to what they said.

FALLACIES IN LOGIC

The style of a speaker is certainly important insofar as it contributes to maintaining the listener's attention. However, style is not a substitute for content, nor is cleverness a substitute for significance. There are a number of rhetorical devices that can be used by a speaker to gain and hold the attention of the listener. Catchy phrases and humorous anecdotes make a speech appealing to listen to, and are certainly not to be condemned. But as a discerning listener, you may want to ask yourself, "Is the speaker using clever rhetoric to avoid confronting the issue directly?" Look for smoke screens, which are designed to conceal rather than illuminate the speaker's meaning. Here are a few questions you can keep in mind to help you perceive what are called *fallacies in logic.*

1 *Is the speaker directing attention away from the real issue?* If the arguments on the issue are weak, the speaker may introduce a *red herring* as a diversionary tactic. The origin of this term is obscure, but it means to associate the issue in question with one that is irrelevant but more emotionally charged. The speaker may begin talking about the evils of social security, labor unions, or the diminishing oil supply and move skillfully into a discourse on the threat of communism, without the audience perceiving what has been done.

2 *Is the speaker's intention to incite the audience with emotionally loaded "trigger words"?* Political speakers occasionally incorporate such terms as "irresponsible hippies" or "misguided bleeding hearts" as a means of gaining favor for themselves by attacking what they know the audience dislikes. This is a tactic called *ad populum* and was used effectively in the 1930s by Adolf Hitler, not as a means of dealing with real problems, but as an avenue to gaining personal power. His relentless tirades against the Jews and the Bolsheviks were effective because the prejudices of the people already existed.

3 *Is the speaker addressing only the weaker assertions of the opposition?* He or she may be setting up a *straw man*—that is, a flimsy argument that can easily be rebutted. The evidence presented may appear strong and convincing, but it may not in fact confront the most significant aspect of the issue. For example, an opponent of capital punishment may attack its supporters by saying they want to execute people because it is cheaper than holding them in prison. Arguing against that position is easier than dealing with the issue of deterrence.

4 *Is the speaker unfairly attacking the character of the opponent?* This is a tactic that is commonly referred to as "mud slinging" and known over the centuries in the Latin phrase *ad hominem.* Again, it is a method used by a protagonist to divert attention away from the issue and onto personal qualities of the opponent. Charges that a candidate drinks too much, swears, or does not go to church say nothing about that person's views or capabilities, but such charges do influence votes. The *ad hominem* attack was used effectively against Governor Nelson Rockefeller when he was campaigning for the 1964 Republican presidential nomination. Opponents cast aspersions upon his ability to govern because of his recent divorce. Another example of the same tactic was directed at Senator Thomas Eagleton in the 1972 presidential campaign. Charges that he had suffered a nervous breakdown caused him to be dropped from the Democratic ticket.

5 *Is the speaker asking for acceptance of an assertion without giving evidence to support it?* This is a fallacy in logic called *begging the question.* Usually it is used in conjunction with a "hooker" designed to reach the listener's emotions or sense of status. A speaker might use this kind of ploy:

> *Anyone with political sophistication knows that civil disobedience is a clear danger to society.*

We all want to think we are politically sophisticated, and it sounds as if in order to be so, we must accept the assertion. Henry David Thoreau and Mahatma Gandhi might disagree, however, and insist on evidence for the claim. But speakers who think they can get away with it may try. It is certainly easier to "beg the question" than to produce proof.

6 *Is the speaker using a "circular argument"?* This is an argument that is used as proof of itself. For example, basing a claim that the Bible is the word of God on statements that are made in the Bible would be a circular argument. One student who was contending that marijuana should not be legalized because it was harmful finally came around to the argument that its harm lay in the possibility of arrest—since it was illegal. The circular argument sounds as if it would be easy to detect, but when it is skillfully concealed in rhetoric it is often difficult to spot.

7 *Is the speaker talking in broad generalities, without being specific?* In making this evaluation we must remember that in all controversies there is never enough evidence. In fact, if all the evidence were available the issue would probably not be controversial. There are times, however, when the lack of essential supporting data can make an argument unacceptable. Here are a few commonly expressed generalizations:

> *Politics is a dirty business. Nobody in Washington is really honest. They're all looking out for their own special interests. They don't vote for what they think is right; they vote the way lobbyists tell them to. The organization that has the strongest lobby is always going to get its way.*

Count the number of unsupported allegations. In all likelihood the speaker would be unable to name a member of Congress who is dishonest or who does not vote for what he or she thinks is right, or to name a lobby that always gets its way. You can avoid the charge of insufficient evidence if you make it a point to have at least one example for every assertion you make.

Another aspect of this fallacy relates to attitudes rather than arguments. People who operate on the basis of stereotypes think that they already have all the facts needed in order to make a judgment. Such persons may never actually make the statement that all fat people are jolly, or all Latins are passionate, or all the Irish are quick-tempered, or all Communists are treacherous. However, stereotypic statements are based on the implicit assumption that they are unquestionable truths.

8 *Is the speaker making unreasonable extrapolations?* Extrapolation is an inference that what has started in the past and continues in the present can reasonably be expected to continue into the future. Some amount of extrapolation is a necessary part of our functioning. We infer that the sun will rise tomorrow, since it has come up every morning in the past. However, extrapolation beyond a reasonable point loses its validity. We may be able to predict the total population next year, or even in thirty years—*provided* the rate of growth follows our computations. Extrapolation is based on the continuation of a present trend or rate. Hence it is valid only up to the point where we can safely assume that this trend will persist unchanged. A business might be safe in planning on the basis of sales figures extrapolated over the next three months, but, given all the vagaries of the economy, a prediction of what its sales will be ten years from now would be sheer conjecture.

Debaters have sometimes been charged with concentrating on argumentation at the expense of truth. Truth is, of course, the prime consideration in the discipline of speech. From a purely practical standpoint, however, the debater learns to avoid faulty reasoning as being destructive to his or her own case. You will have to test any evidence you present just as the debater does. It is your responsibility both as a speaker and as a listener to be able to distinguish between sound and faulty reasoning.

9 *Is the speaker making statements that do not follow in a logical sequence?* Such a statement is called a *non sequitur—* a Latin term meaning "not in sequence." In other words a speaker may be making a leap in logic without linking the conclusion to the preceding statement. There may be a relationship, but too many steps have been left out for there to be a clear connection. For example, you might hear a speaker say this:

Since we live in a democracy, our health care is the best in the world.

The attempt here was to discredit socialized medicine by tying it to a form of government. The speaker wants you to think that politics and health care are inextricably interwoven and that to change one is to change the other. It is difficult, of course, to avoid every element of the non sequitur without getting hopelessly bogged down in awkward detail, but you should be able to recognize the gross violations.

As you can tell from this list of fallacies, the process of critical listening is closely related to the process of thinking and reasoning. As you study and learn more about the art of public communication you will sharpen your skill not only in sending and receiving messages, but in thinking clearly about issues and arriving at rational conclusions. Most of what you believe to be true is acquired by your accepting what you are told by others. In a complex society such as ours you are bombarded continuously by a barrage of words which urge you to buy, sell, vote, and behave in a variety of ways. You are exposed to more information than you can possibly process—some of it valuable, much of it useless or counterproductive. Out of it all you must be able to draw some conclusions that you can use yourself when you become the sender of messages.

QUESTIONS FOR DISCUSSION

1   Do you consider yourself to be a good listener? What are the things you do that make your listening effective? What are the faults in your listening?

2   Do you think that most people are able to recognize fallacies in logic? Would you consider it ethical to use logical fallacies to convince someone of something you sincerely believed in?

3   Can you convince people they are wrong by pointing out fallacies in their logic? Is it possible to recognize a fallacy and still believe the argument to be true?

SUGGESTED ACTIVITIES

1   Pair up with another member of the class. Have one person give directions to the other on how to do something without the receiver making any comment or asking any questions. Then have the receiver repeat the directions as they were perceived. Check with the sender to see if the message was received accurately.

2   Write a proverb that you believe to be true. Cite an example from your own experience that reinforces it. Ask the rest of the class if they agree with the proverb.

3   Write a proverb to which you take exception. Give examples from your own experience that support your objection.

4   Write an original proverb.

INDEX

Microphones, 91–92
Model of communication, 4
Modes of proof, 60–63
Motion-picture projector, 91
Mud slinging, 140

Narration, 37–38
New York Times Index, 26
Nichols, Ralph, 132
Non sequitur, 142
Nonverbal communication, 6, 97
Note cards, 86–87

Opaque projector, 90
Oratorical emphasis, 111
Oratory, 4
Organization of speech (see Outlining)
Outlining:
  examples of, 55–56, 75–76
  final draft in, 54–55
  patterns of, 49–50
  rough draft in, 46–54
Overhead projector, 90
Overt response of audience, 105–106

Pathos, 61–62
Patterns of organization, 49–50
Pericles, 3
Persuasion, 59–77
Persuasive information, 64–65
Phonograph, 90
Physical materials for speaking,
  preparation of, 86–92
Pitch of voice, 98–99
Pointer phrase, 110–111
Political sentiments of audience, 126–127
Porter, Sylvia, 132–133
Posture, 6, 96
Prejudiced audience, 119–120
Presummary, 47–48

Prima facie case, 75–77
Primary messages, 6
Progressive relaxation, 82
Projections in testimonial evidence, 36
Proof, modes of, 60–63
Protagoras, 4
Psychological Abstracts, 27
Psychological preparation for speaking,
  80–83
Purpose statements, 18–20, 47–48

Quality of information, 28
Question period, 103–105
Quotations, 51

Radio, 91
Rate of delivery, 99–100
Readers' Guide to Periodical Literature,
  26
Reading from manuscript, 83
Reasoning:
  deductive, 68–69
  inductive, 67–68
Red herring, 139
Reference works, 27
Religious beliefs of audience, 127–128
Repetition, 110
Research material, 26
Respect for audience, 128–129
Response from audience, 105–107
Retentive listening, 136–138
Rhetoric, 2
Rhetorical question, 52
Rhetorical transition, 100
Rogers, Carl, 135

St. Augustine, 111
Secondary messages, 6
Semantics, 6, 30
Signs in inductive reasoning, 68
Sincerity of speaker, 102